Azure PowerShell Quick Start Guide

Deploy and manage Azure virtual machines with ease

Thomas Mitchell

BIRMINGHAM - MUMBAI

Azure PowerShell Quick Start Guide

Commissioning Editor: Vijin Boricha
Acquisition Editor: Reshma Raman
Content Development Editor: Roshan Kumar
Technical Editor: Shweta Jadhav
Copy Editor: Safis Editing
Project Coordinator: Namrata Swetta
Proofreader: Safis Editing
Indexer: Priyanka Dhadke
Graphics: Jason Monteiro
Production Coordinator: Nilesh Mohite

First published: December 2018

Production reference: 1191218

Published by Packt Publishing Ltd.
Livery Place
35 Livery Street
Birmingham
B3 2PB, UK.

ISBN 978-1-78961-495-4

www.packtpub.com

`mapt.io`

Mapt is an online digital library that gives you full access to over 5,000 books and videos, as well as industry leading tools to help you plan your personal development and advance your career. For more information, please visit our website.

Why subscribe?

- Spend less time learning and more time coding with practical eBooks and Videos from over 4,000 industry professionals

- Improve your learning with Skill Plans built especially for you

- Get a free eBook or video every month

- Mapt is fully searchable

- Copy and paste, print, and bookmark content

Packt.com

Did you know that Packt offers eBook versions of every book published, with PDF and ePub files available? You can upgrade to the eBook version at `www.packt.com` and as a print book customer, you are entitled to a discount on the eBook copy. Get in touch with us at `customercare@packtpub.com` for more details.

At `www.packt.com`, you can also read a collection of free technical articles, sign up for a range of free newsletters, and receive exclusive discounts and offers on Packt books and eBooks.

Contributors

About the author

Thomas Mitchell is a 25+ year veteran of the IT industry and carries numerous industry certifications. He has built a rather in-depth skill set that spans numerous IT disciplines. Tom's disciplines include Microsoft Exchange, Microsoft Office 365, Microsoft Azure, and Active Directory. He is now an independent IT consultant, a freelance author, and online IT trainer, has written about numerous IT topics for several online publications, and has even published several of his own IT courses on *Udemy (dot) com*.

You can find a complete list of his courses at *thomasmitchell (dot) net/udemy*. Tom is the managing editor for *understandingazure (dot) com*. He lives with his wife, Darlene, and five kids, Michael, Tommy, Joey, Brittany, and Matthew.

I would like to thank Packt for all the contributions for the book. Reshma Raman and Roshan Kumar were immensely helpful to me, they both provided invaluable feedback to make the book better. I would like to thank my technical reviewers and proofreaders for their thorough reviews and insightful comments. I'd like to thank my wife and kids for dealing with the long hours that I've spent in front of my laptop. Part of my drive while writing this book was that the completion of this book would demonstrate to my kids that effort is rewarded.

About the reviewer

Anders Eide, manager at KPMG, loves his job as it lets him make the right decisions with customers, combined with the eagerness to always be at the cutting edge of innovative technologies. This love for new technology and new ways of thinking is also one of the reasons he as been awarded as Microsoft Azure MVP since 2014.

Packt is searching for authors like you

If you're interested in becoming an author for Packt, please visit `authors.packtpub.com` and apply today. We have worked with thousands of developers and tech professionals, just like you, to help them share their insight with the global tech community. You can make a general application, apply for a specific hot topic that we are recruiting an author for, or submit your own idea.

Table of Contents

Preface

The world is racing to the cloud. As such, it's critical that IT professionals stay ahead of the curve by learning about all that the cloud has to offer. Those professionals that do not will find themselves sidelined as a new breed of engineers emerges—a breed that speaks cloud proficiently. Because *cloud* is such a broad term, I chose to focus on Microsoft Azure in this book. More specifically, I chose to focus on how PowerShell (another little-understood technology) can be used to deploy and manage **virtual machines** (**VM**) in Microsoft Azure. By doing so, I was able to produce a book that provides current IT professionals with a *roadmap*, if you will, for learning PowerShell and Azure skills that many other IT professionals do not possess.

Who this book is for

This book is for any IT professional who wants a solid guide for learning practical Azure and PowerShell skills. While this book does cover technologies that you may not be intimately familiar with, the structure of the book, coupled with the guided labs, offers an opportunity to have fun while learning.

Because the book focuses on deploying and managing Azure VMs entirely with PowerShell, numerous PowerShell commands are featured throughout the book. However, only basic knowledge of PowerShell is required to run them.

What this book covers

Chapter 1, *Getting Started*, covers the basics of Azure PowerShell and introduces you to basic PowerShell tasks, including the installation of Azure PowerShell and how to connect to Azure with it. It also covers remedial tasks, such as deploying a VM in Azure with PowerShell, resizing a VM, and managing VM states—all with PowerShell.

Chapter 2, *Working with Images*, introduces a few image-related Azure tasks that can be completed with PowerShell. It discusses the deployment of VMs using PowerShell with Marketplace images as well as how to create custom images and how to deploy VMs from such custom images.

Chapter 3, *Working with Disks*, covers more advanced topics, including the deployment and attachment of data disks using PowerShell. Also covered in this chapter is the creation of VM snapshots, and how to deploy new VMs from such snapshots. Encryption of VMs and virtual disks is also covered.

Chapter 4, *High Availability*, explores the deployment of availability sets and how to load balance Azure VMs.

Chapter 5, *Other Cool Stuff*, explores various other cool tricks that you can do with Azure PowerShell. Covered in this chapter is the creation and attachment of NICs to VMs using PowerShell. Tagging VMs with PowerShell and redeploying VMs with PowerShell are also covered, as are admin password resets. However, the coolest topic covered in this chapter is the management of VMs with custom script extensions.

To get the most out of this book

This book is intended for IT professionals who are responsible for managing Azure VMs. No prior PowerShell or Azure experience is needed.

Download the color images

We also provide a PDF file that has color images of the screenshots/diagrams used in this book. You can download it here: https://www.packtpub.com/sites/default/files/downloads/9781789614954_ColorImages.pdf.

Conventions used

There are a number of text conventions used throughout this book.

CodeInText: Indicates code words in text, database table names, folder names, filenames, file extensions, pathnames, dummy URLs, user input, and Twitter handles. Here is an example: "Mount the downloaded WebStorm-10*.dmg disk image file as another disk in your system."

Any command-line input or output is written as follows:

```
$myVnet = Get-AzureRmVirtualNetwork `
 -Name "myVnet" `
 -ResourceGroupName "VMLab"
$subnet = $myVnet.Subnets|?{$_.Name -eq 'mySubnet'}
```

Bold: Indicates a new term, an important word, or words that you see onscreen. For example, words in menus or dialog boxes appear in the text like this. Here is an example: "Select **System info** from the **Administration** panel."

Warnings or important notes appear like this.

Tips and tricks appear like this.

Get in touch

Feedback from our readers is always welcome.

General feedback: If you have questions about any aspect of this book, mention the book title in the subject of your message and email us at customercare@packtpub.com.

Errata: Although we have taken every care to ensure the accuracy of our content, mistakes do happen. If you have found a mistake in this book, we would be grateful if you would report this to us. Please visit www.packt.com/submit-errata, selecting your book, clicking on the Errata Submission Form link, and entering the details.

Piracy: If you come across any illegal copies of our works in any form on the Internet, we would be grateful if you would provide us with the location address or website name. Please contact us at copyright@packt.com with a link to the material.

If you are interested in becoming an author: If there is a topic that you have expertise in and you are interested in either writing or contributing to a book, please visit authors.packtpub.com.

Reviews

Please leave a review. Once you have read and used this book, why not leave a review on the site that you purchased it from? Potential readers can then see and use your unbiased opinion to make purchase decisions, we at Packt can understand what you think about our products, and our authors can see your feedback on their book. Thank you!

For more information about Packt, please visit packt.com.

Getting Started 1

Welcome to the basics! In this chapter, we will start things off at the ground level. Basic PowerShell tasks will be covered so that you learn some basic concepts before going into more complex tasks. Before attempting any exercises covered in this book, you should first complete the ones covered in this chapter.

In this chapter, we will cover the following topics:

- Installing Azure PowerShell
- Deploying a virtual machine (VM)
- Resizing a VM with PowerShell
- VM power states
- Basic management tasks

At the end of this chapter, you will have the opportunity to practice what you've learned by completing a hands-on exercise that covers many of the basic tasks covered in this chapter.

Installing Azure PowerShell

Performing management tasks within an Azure tenant, using PowerShell, requires a handful of prerequisites to be met first. For example, the AzureRM PowerShell module needs to be installed so that Azure PowerShell commands become available. However, since the preferred method of installing the AzureRM module is to do so via the PowerShell Gallery, the latest version of `PowerShellGet` needs to be installed first.

Once the latest versions of `PowerShellGet` and AzureRM are installed, the AzureRM module can be loaded and used to connect to the Azure tenant. The next few exercises will walk you through the installation of `PowerShellGet`, how to use it to download and install AzureRM, and then how to use AzureRM to connect to an Azure tenant.

Installing PowerShellGet

Before using PowerShell to deploy and manage virtual machines in Azure, you will need to install the Azure PowerShell module (AzureRM) on your workstation. The best way to install Azure PowerShell is to do it from the PowerShell Gallery, which is what you will learn to do in this section, starting with the installation of `PowerShellGet`.

The installation of `PowerShellGet` is necessary because `PowerShellGet` is the tool that is used to pull down PowerShell modules from the gallery—so, before doing anything, you need to ensure that you have the latest version of the `PowerShellGet` module (https://www.powershellgallery.com/) installed on your workstation. To check what version of `PowerShellGet` you have, run the `Get-Module` command, which is shown as follows:

```
Get-Module `
 -Name PowerShellGet `
 -ListAvailable | Select-Object -Property Name,Version,Path
```

The `Get-Module` command will list what versions of PowerShellGet are currently available on your workstation. By piping the results of the `Get-Module` command (using the |
character) to the `Select-Object` command, you can view just the info you are looking for. In this case, you can see the **Name**, **Version**, and **Path** of each instance of `PowerShellGet` that currently resides on your machine:

```
Windows PowerShell
Copyright (C) Microsoft Corporation. All rights reserved.

PS C:\Users\tmitchell> Get-Module -Name PowerShellGet -ListAvailable | Select-Object -Property Name,Version,Path

Name           Version Path
----           ------- ----
PowerShellGet 1.6.5   C:\Program Files\WindowsPowerShell\Modules\PowerShellGet\1.6.5\PowerShellGet.psd1
PowerShellGet 1.6.0   C:\Program Files\WindowsPowerShell\Modules\PowerShellGet\1.6.0\PowerShellGet.psd1
PowerShellGet 1.0.0.1 C:\Program Files\WindowsPowerShell\Modules\PowerShellGet\1.0.0.1\PowerShellGet.psd1

PS C:\Users\tmitchell>
```

To perform the exercises in this book, you are going to need `PowerShellGet` version 1.1.2.0 or later installed. If you don't have `PowerShellGet` version 1.1.2.0 or later installed, update it by running the `Install-Module` command, shown as follows:

```
Install-Module PowerShellGet -Force
```

The `Install-Module` command will update your `PowerShellGet` module to the latest version. Specifying the `-Force` switch simply suppresses any `Are you sure?` confirmation type messages. The following screenshot shows the installation of `PowerShellGet`:

```
Windows PowerShell
Copyright (C) Microsoft Corporation. All rights reserved.

Installing package 'PowerShellGet'
    Installed dependent package 'PackageManagement'
    [oooooooooooooooooooooooooooooooooooooooooooooooooooooooooooooooooooooooooooo                                ]

PowerShellGet 1.6.5   C:\Program Files\WindowsPowerShell\Modules\PowerShellGet\1.6.5\PowerShellGet.psd1
PowerShellGet 1.6.0   C:\Program Files\WindowsPowerShell\Modules\PowerShellGet\1.6.0\PowerShellGet.psd1
PowerShellGet 1.0.0.1 C:\Program Files\WindowsPowerShell\Modules\PowerShellGet\1.0.0.1\PowerShellGet.psd1


PS C:\Users\tmitchell> Install-Module PowerShellGet -Force
```

Once the latest version of `PowerShellGet` is installed, you can install Azure PowerShell.

Installing the Azure PowerShell module

Before using `PowerShellGet` to download and install Azure PowerShell, you must first configure your PowerShell environment with an execution policy that allows scripts to run. Since the default execution policy for PowerShell is **Restricted**, you must change it by running the `Set-ExecutionPolicy` command:

```
Set-ExecutionPolicy -ExecutionPolicy RemoteSigned
```

Running the `Set-ExecutionPolicy` command, to set the execution policy to `RemoteSigned`, is sufficient for installing Azure PowerShell from the PowerShell Gallery. You could also set your policy to **Unrestricted**, but that would further open you up to unsigned commands that could be malicious. As you can see in the following screenshot, PowerShell will prompt you to confirm that you wish to change the execution policy:

```
Execution Policy Change
The execution policy helps protect you from scripts that you do not trust. Changing the execution policy might expose you to the security risks
described in the about Execution Policies help topic at https:/go.microsoft.com/fwlink/?LinkID=135170. Do you want to change the execution policy?
[Y] Yes [A] Yes to All [N] No [L] No to All [S] Suspend [?] Help (default is "N"): y
```

Once your execution policy is set to **RemoteSigned**, you can install the AzureRM PowerShell module by running the `Install-Module` command:

```
Install-Module -Name AzureRM -AllowClobber
```

Running the preceding command launches the process of connecting to the PowerShell Gallery and downloading the Azure PowerShell module. The `AllowClobber` switch ensures that you get the full and complete installation of AzureRM.

As you can see in the following screenshot, the PowerShell Gallery is not configured as a trusted repository for `PowerShellGet` (you'd think it would be trusted by default). As such, you are likely to see a warning about the repository not being trusted, and you will be prompted whether you are sure you want to download the module. It's safe to answer **Yes**, or **Yes to all**, when you see this prompt.

Selecting **Yes** allows the installation of Azure PowerShell to continue:

```
Untrusted repository
You are installing the modules from an untrusted repository. If you trust this repository, change its InstallationPolicy value by running the
Set-PSRepository cmdlet. Are you sure you want to install the modules from 'PSGallery'?
[Y] Yes  [A] Yes to All  [N] No  [L] No to All  [S] Suspend  [?] Help (default is "N"):
```

The installation of Azure PowerShell is generally painless. The AzureRM module that gets installed is a rollup module for the Azure Resource Manager `cmdlets`. Installing the AzureRM module also pulls down, from the PowerShell Gallery, any Azure PowerShell module not previously installed.

Loading the AzureRM module

Once the Azure PowerShell module (AzureRM) has been installed, you can load the module into your PowerShell session using the `Import-Module` command. As per Microsoft's recommendations, you should do this in a non-elevated PowerShell session, so if you haven't done so already, open a new *non-elevated* PowerShell session and, from within this session, run the following command:

```
Import-Module -Name AzureRM
```

Importing the Azure PowerShell module is rather uneventful. However, rest assured that, unless an error message is displayed, you now have Azure PowerShell loaded—and now that you have Azure PowerShell installed and loaded, you can now actually connect to Azure using PowerShell.

Connecting to Azure via PowerShell

Although Azure PowerShell supports multiple login methods, the easiest way to get logged in is interactively at the command line, using the `Connect-AzureRMAccount` command. It's a simple command to run:

```
Connect-AzureRmAccount
```

After hitting *Enter*, a dialog box prompts you for your Azure admin credentials. Go ahead and supply your Azure admin credentials. Once you've supplied those credentials, you will be connected to your tenant:

To confirm that you are connected to your Azure tenant, you can run the `Get-AzureRmSubscription` command from PowerShell to confirm that it returns your subscription information:

```
Get-AzureRmSubscription
```

If the preceding command returns your subscription info, you can move on to the next steps.

Deploying a virtual machine (VM)

The objective of this section is to walk you through the process of deploying a VM in Azure, using PowerShell. Topics covered in this section include the provisioning of a resource group and the deployment of a VM.

Since the deployment of a VM in Azure, using PowerShell, requires quite a few switches to be specified, each switch will also be explained in detail.

Creating a resource group

Before deploying a VM in Azure with PowerShell, you need to first create a resource group into which the VM will be deployed. An Azure resource group, by the way, is a logical container into which Azure resources are deployed and from where they are managed. Deploying a resource group is rather easy; it is completed with just a single PowerShell command.

To provision a group, you just need to run the `New-AzureRMResourceGroup` command. When running the command, you need to specify a name for the resource group and a location for it:

```
New-AzureRmResourceGroup -ResourceGroupName "VMLab" -Location "EastUS"
```

In the preceding example, I'm specifying the `ResourceGroupName` and `Location` switches. The preceding command creates a resource group called `VMLab` and it creates it in the `EastUS` location:

```
PS C:\Users\tmitchell> New-AzureRmResourceGroup -ResourceGroupName "VMLab" -Location "EastUS"


ResourceGroupName : VMLab
Location          : eastus
ProvisioningState : Succeeded
Tags              :
ResourceId        : /subscriptions/4eacb230-3e94-4bec-9cb8-2a5be79fb60e/resourceGroups/VMLab



PS C:\Users\tmitchell>
```

Running the `New-AzureRMResourceGroup` command takes just a moment or two and, once the command completes, you can visit the Azure dashboard to confirm that the resource group has been created. Instead, you can run the `Get-AzureRmResourceGroup` PowerShell command without any switches, to ensure that the new resource group is listed.

To confirm that your new `VMLab` resource group has been created, run the following command:

```
Get-AzureRmResourceGroup
```

Upon running the preceding command, you should see a resource group called `VMLab` listed. Before continuing with the next exercises (if you are following along), be sure that you've created a resource group, called `VMLab`.

Provisioning a VM with PowerShell

When creating a VM, several options are available to you—including OS image, network configuration, and administrative credentials. However, a VM can also be created with default settings, using a minimal configuration.

The process of provisioning a VM consists of two different PowerShell commands. The first command, called `Get-Credential`, allows you to specify local administrator credentials for the VM. Once those credentials have been established, you can run the `New-AzureRmVm` command to configure and deploy a VM.

To create a local admin account and password for the VM being deployed, run the following command:

```
$cred = Get-Credential
```

This command results in a prompt, to which you can respond, by supplying a local admin account login and associated password. The login information provided in the prompt is then used by the VM deployment process to provision a local admin for the VM when it is deployed:

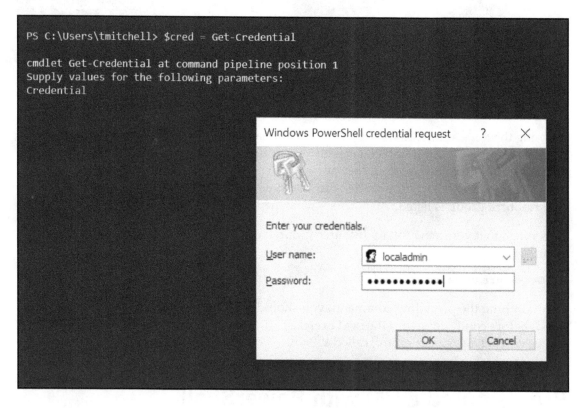

Running the `$cred = Get-Credential` command stores the local admin credentials that you provide in the `$cred` variable. After creating the local admin credentials, you can run the `New-AzureRmVm` command to provision the VM.

The `$cred` variable is referenced during the provisioning process, so that when the VM is provisioned, the local admin info that was provided is used.

To provision a new VM, run the entire following command in a PowerShell session:

```
New-AzureRmVm -ResourceGroupName "VMLab" `
  -Name "myVM" `
  -Location "EastUS" `
  -VirtualNetworkName "myVnet" `
  -SubnetName "mySubnet" `
```

```
-SecurityGroupName "myNSG" `
-PublicIpAddressName "myPublicIP" `
-Credential $cred
```

The preceding command is a single-line command. Although the command itself is broken up into multiple lines, this command is one long command when written out.

To break the command up into multiple lines so that I can better explain it, I used the *tick* symbol (`) to let PowerShell know it's one long command, despite being supplied over multiple lines.

If you prefer the copy/paste approach, visit `mybook.thomasmitchell.net` for an online version of all the commands in this book:

The *tick* symbol tells PowerShell that even though I'm supplying a multi-line command, it should be interpreted as a single-line command instead.

With that said, let's go through the command, line by line.

As you can see from the preceding command (which takes about 10-15 minutes to run), `New-AzurermVM` requires some basic information to provision a VM.

The `ResourceGroupName` switch tells the command which resource group the VM should be deployed to. In this case, the VM is going to be deployed into the VMLab resource group that was provisioned earlier (if you are following along with these instructions).
The `Name` switch specifies the name of the VM being deployed. In this example, the VM is going to be called `myVM`.

The new VM is deployed into the `EastUS` region by specifying the `Location` switch.

Since the VM needs to go onto a network and subnet, this command includes the `VirtualNetworkName` switch and `SubnetName` switch. In the preceding example, the VM is being deployed to a virtual network called `myVNet` and a subnet called `mySubnet`. Because we haven't created a virtual network yet, nor a subnet, the `New-AzureRmVM` command is going to create them automatically, using default IP range values. Had we previously provisioned a virtual network and virtual subnet, we could specify their names instead, and the VM would be deployed to them.

To protect the VM, a network security group needs to be deployed. To provision and associate a network security group with the new VM, the `SecurityGroupName` switch is used. In the preceding example, the network security group is called `myNSG`. As was the case with the virtual network and virtual subnet, had we pre-provisioned another security group, we could have specified that group with the `SecurityGroupName` switch.

To be able to RDP to the new VM over the internet from a workstation, we need to give the VM a public IP address. This is done with the `PublicIPAddressName` switch. In this example, the public IP address resource is called `myPublicIP`.

In a production environment, assigning a public IP address and enabling RDP for a VM is a terrible practice. You never want to make RDP available over the internet on a production machine. I'm simply enabling RDP in this case for ease of use, so I can more easily work through the deployment process.

With that PSA out of the way, we must tell the `New-AzureRmVm` command what local admin credentials to provision for this VM. To do this, I'm specifying the `Credential` switch and referencing the `$cred` variable with it.

With all this information provided, running the `New-AzureRmVm` command will deploy a default Windows 2016 Server into the EastUS region, onto a new subnet called mySubnet, which is part of a virtual network called `myVnet`. The VM will be protected by a default set of rules contained in a network security group called `MyNSG`.

The VM deployed with the preceding command is called `myVM` and it will be deployed into a resource group called `VMLab`. It will assign a dynamic public IP address that is accessible from the internet and the local admin account, which will match what was configured when we ran the `Get-Credential` command:

```
ResourceGroupName        : VMLab
Id                       : /subscriptions/4eacb230-3e94-4bec-9cb8-2a5be79fb60e/resourceGroups/VMLab/providers/Microsoft.Compute/virtualMachines/myVM
VmId                     : afdfbc14-2d22-450c-9b57-aa11e41b4a46
Name                     : myVM
Type                     : Microsoft.Compute/virtualMachines
Location                 : eastus
Tags                     : {}
HardwareProfile          : {VmSize}
NetworkProfile           : {NetworkInterfaces}
OSProfile                : {ComputerName, AdminUsername, WindowsConfiguration, Secrets}
ProvisioningState        : Succeeded
StorageProfile           : {ImageReference, OsDisk, DataDisks}
FullyQualifiedDomainName  : myvm-140b09.EastUS.cloudapp.azure.com
```

The VM deployment process can take several minutes to complete, but when it does, you will have a fully functioning virtual machine deployed.

Once the deployment is complete, you can confirm in the Azure dashboard that the VM is up and running. You can also run the following command instead:

```
Get-AzureRmVm -resourcegroup VMLab -name MyVM -status
```

The output of the preceding command will show the status of your newly deployed VM.

Connecting to a VM with RDP from PowerShell

Since the intention of this book is to explain how to deploy and manage VMs using PowerShell, it makes sense to explain how to RDP to a VM from PowerShell.

Once a VM is deployed, you can create a remote desktop connection with the VM right from a PowerShell session. To do so, you need to run two commands.

First, you need to track down the public IP address of the VM by running the `Get-AzureRmPublicIpAddress` command. This command will display the public IP address of the VM. You can then use that IP to connect to the VM.

To obtain the IP address of the `MyVM` VM deployed in the preceding example, run the following command:

```
Get-AzureRmPublicIpAddress `
 -Name myPublicIP `
 -ResourceGroupName VMLab | Select IPAddress
```

The `Get-AzureRmPublicIpAddress` command displays the public IP address for the VM. All you have to do is tell the command which public IP resource you want to query and then pipe that data to a `Select` statement:

```
PS C:\Users\tmitchell> Get-AzureRmPublicIpAddress -Name myPublicIP -ResourceGroupName VMLab | Select IPAddress

IpAddress
---------
40.121.34.164
```

The output is the public IP address of the VM.

To connect to the VM via RDP, you can run the `mstsc.exe` command right from the PowerShell session and replace `publicIpAddress` with the IP address of the VM:

```
mstsc.exe /v:publicIpAddress
```

In the Windows Security window, supply the local username and password that you created for the VM and then click **OK**:

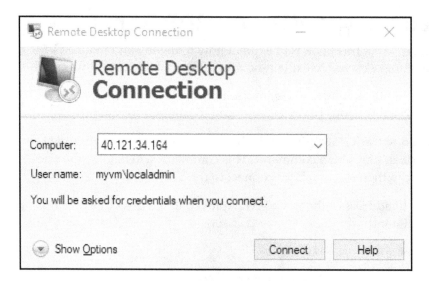

The RDP client session will launch and then you can log into the newly provisioned VM. Logging into the new virtual machine from this point forward is no different from any other RDP session.

Resizing a VM with PowerShell

There will be times when an application will require more resources than it once did. In cases such as these, an Azure VM can be resized.

Resizing a VM requires the use of two different PowerShell commands. The first command, called `Get-AzureRmVMSize`, is used to retrieve a list of VM sizes available in a chosen region. Before resizing a virtual machine, you must ensure that whatever size you want to change the virtual machine to is available in the virtual machine's region. The `Get-AzureRmVMSize` command does exactly this.

The second command that is required the `Update-AzureRmVM` command. This command is used to update a VM after changing its size configuration.

Resizing a VM

In this section, you are going to resize the `myVM` virtual machine that you created earlier. However, before attempting to do so, you will need to retrieve a list of VM sizes available in the `EastUS` region, which is where the `myVM` virtual machine resides.

To complete this task, run the following command from PowerShell:

```
Get-AzureRmVMSize -Location "EastUS"
```

The preceding command should return quite a few sizes. Confirm that `Standard DS2_V2` is available. If it's not, find another size that is available.

After confirming that `Standard DS2_V2` (or your chosen size) is available, you can use PowerShell to resize the `myVM` virtual machine:

```
PS C:\Users\tmitchell> Get-AzureRmVMSize -Location "EastUS"

Name              NumberOfCores  MemoryInMB  MaxDataDiskCount  OSDiskSizeInMB  ResourceDiskSizeInMB
----              -------------  ----------  ----------------  --------------  --------------------
Standard_B1ms                1        2048                 2         1047552                  4096
Standard_B1s                 1        1024                 2         1047552                  2048
Standard_B2ms                2        8192                 4         1047552                 16384
Standard_B2s                 2        4096                 4         1047552                  8192
Standard_B4ms                4       16384                 8         1047552                 32768
Standard_B8ms                8       32768                16         1047552                 65536
Standard_DS1_v2              1        3584                 4         1047552                  7168
Standard_DS2_v2              2        7168                 8         1047552                 14336
```

After confirming that `Standard DS2_V2` is available in the `EastUS` region, you also need to make sure that it's available on the current cluster where the `myVM` virtual machine resides. To do so, use the same `Get-AzureRmVMSize` command as before—just with a few different switches.

To confirm that the `Standard DS2_V2` size (or your chosen size) is available on the cluster where `myVM` resides, run the following command:

```
Get-AzureRmVMSize -ResourceGroupName "VMLab" -VMName "myVM"
```

By specifying the `-VMName` and `-ResourceGroupName` switches in the preceding command, you can confirm that the `Standard DS2_V2` size is available on the same cluster as the VM. If so, the virtual machine can be resized from a powered-on state (without the need to deallocate it). However, it will still require a reboot during the operation:

```
PS C:\Users\tmitchell> Get-AzureRmVMSize -ResourceGroupName "VMLab" -VMName "myVM"

Name          NumberOfCores MemoryInMB MaxDataDiskCount OSDiskSizeInMB ResourceDiskSizeInMB
----          ------------- ---------- ---------------- -------------- --------------------
Standard_B1ms             1       2048                2        1047552                 4096
Standard_B1s              1       1024                2        1047552                 2048
Standard_B2ms             2       8192                4        1047552                16384
Standard_B2s              2       4096                4        1047552                 8192
Standard_B4ms             4      16384                8        1047552                32768
Standard_B8ms             8      32768               16        1047552                65536
Standard_A0               1        768                1        1047552                20480
Standard_A1               1       1792                2        1047552                71680
Standard_A2               2       3584                4        1047552               138240
Standard_A3               4       7168                8        1047552               291840
Standard_A5               2      14336                4        1047552               138240
Standard_A4               8      14336               16        1047552               619520
Standard_A6               4      28672                8        1047552               291840
Standard_A7               8      57344               16        1047552               619520
```

If the `Standard DS2_V2` size is not available on the VM's current cluster, the virtual machine needs to first be deallocated before the resize operation can occur. In such a case, any data on the temp disk is removed and the public IP address will change (unless a static IP address is being used).

To resize the virtual machine (`myVM`), you need to run a few different PowerShell commands.

The first command essentially loads the configuration profile of the VM into a variable called `$vm`. The second command will modify the `-VMSize` attribute stored in that variable to reflect the new VM size. The third command, called `Update-AzureRmVM`, will take the updated configuration that is stored in the `$vm` variable and write it to the VM.

To begin the resize process of the myVM virtual machine, run the following command from a PowerShell session that's connected to your Azure tenant:

```
$vm = Get-AzureRmVM -ResourceGroupName "VMLab" -VMName "myVM"
```

The preceding command retrieves the current VM information and stores it in the $vm variable.

To modify the size attribute for the VM, run the following command:

```
$vm.HardwareProfile.VmSize = "Standard_DS2_V2"
```

The previous command changes the size attribute of the myVM virtual machine that's stored in the variable to Standard DS2_V2.

Once the new size has been specified using the preceding command, run the following command to update the VM:

```
Update-AzureRmVM -VM $vm -ResourceGroupName "VMLab"
```

After executing the preceding Update-AzureRmVM command, the myVM virtual machine is updated and then automatically restarted:

```
PS C:\Users\tmitchell> Update-AzureRmVM -VM $vm -ResourceGroupName "VMLab"

RequestId IsSuccessStatusCode StatusCode ReasonPhrase
--------- ------------------- ---------- ------------
                        True        OK OK
```

The process takes a few minutes to complete, but when it completes, the myVM virtual machine is resized to reflect the new size.

VM power states

If you manage any number of Azure VMs on a day-to-day basis, you are going to need to understand the different states in which VMs can exist. In this section, I want to briefly touch on the available power states for a VM, and on how to check the current power state of a VMe via PowerShell.

There are seven power states that a VM can exist in:

- **Starting**: Indicates that the VM is being started.
- **Running**: Indicates that the VM is running.
- **Stopping**: Indicates that the VM is being stopped.
- **Stopped**: Indicates that the VM is stopped. Note that VMs in the stopped state still incur compute charges.
- **Deallocating**: Indicates that the VM is being deallocated.
- **Deallocated**: Indicates that the VM is completely removed from the hypervisor but still available in the control plane. VMs in the deallocated state do not incur compute charges.
- **Unknown (–)**: Indicates that the power state of the VM is unknown.

Although most of these are self-explanatory, I wanted to ensure that you were aware of them.

Retrieving the VM's status

Retrieving the status of a VM is rather straightforward. To retrieve the state of a specific virtual machine, use the `Get-AzureRmVM` command, taking care to specify valid names for the VM and the resource group.

Run the following command to check the status of the `myVM` virtual machine:

```
Get-AzureRmVM `
  -ResourceGroupName "VMLab" `
  -Name "myVM" `
  -Status
```

The command in the preceding example retrieves the current status of the `myVM` virtual machine. While the output will include quite a bit of information, what we are most concerned about for this exercise is the part that shows whether the VM is running:

```
ResourceGroupName : VMLab
Name              : myVM
Disks[0]          :
  Name            : myVM_OsDisk_1_c2757511fbf8423ebce7a23e0c297873
  Statuses[0]     :
    Code          : ProvisioningState/succeeded
    Level         : Info
    DisplayStatus : Provisioning succeeded
    Time          : 7/20/2018 7:41:52 PM
VMAgent            :
  VmAgentVersion  : 2.7.41491.875
  Statuses[0]     :
    Code          : ProvisioningState/succeeded
    Level         : Info
    DisplayStatus : Ready
    Message       : GuestAgent is running and accepting new configurations.
    Time          : 7/20/2018 7:42:02 PM
Statuses[0]       :
  Code            : ProvisioningState/succeeded
  Level           : Info
  DisplayStatus   : Provisioning succeeded
  Time            : 7/20/2018 7:43:33 PM
Statuses[1]       :
  Code            : PowerState/running
  Level           : Info
  DisplayStatus   : VM running
```

The resulting output indicates the current status of the VM.

Basic management tasks

Day-to-day operations will often require you to perform several management tasks, such as starting, stopping, and deleting vVMs. In addition, you may find yourself in situations where you will need (or want) to create scripts to automate certain VM tasks.

By becoming familiar with how to use Azure PowerShell, you can script and automate many common management tasks that would otherwise require manual intervention.

The five main commands I'm going to cover in this section are `Stop-AzureRmVM`, `Start-AzureRmVM`, `Restart-AzureRmVM`, `Remove-AzureRmVM`, and `Remove-AzureRmResourceGroup`.

The Stop VM command

To stop an Azure VM, you can use the `Stop-AzureRmVm` command. Go ahead and run the command to stop the `myVM` virtual machine:

```
Stop-AzureRmVm -ResourceGroupName "VMLab" -Name "myVM" -Force
```

The only switches required in the preceding command are the `ResourceGroupName` switch and the `Name` switch. The `Force` switch is optional, but it shuts down the VM without asking for confirmation.

Another optional switch (not shown) is the `StayProvisioned` switch. If you wish to stop a VM but keep the virtual machine allocated, you could specify the `StayProvisioned` switch as well. Keep in mind that if you do this, you will continue to be charged for compute cycles even though the VM is off.

Once you've stopped the `myVM` virtual machine, run the `Get-AzureRmVM` command to confirm the status of it:

```
Get-AzureRmVM `
  -ResourceGroupName "VMLab" `
  -Name "myVM" `
  -Status
```

The preceding command will display the status of the `myVM` virtual machine and should show the status as **Deallocated**:

```
Statuses[1]           :
    Code              : PowerState/deallocated
    Level             : Info
    DisplayStatus     : VM deallocated
```

In the next section, you will start the `myVM` virtual machine, using the `Start-AzureRmVM` command.

The Start VM command

To start a VM, you can use the `Start-AzureRmVM` command. Run the following command to start the `myVM` virtual machine:

```
Start-AzureRmVM -ResourceGroupName "VMLab" -Name "myVM"
```

The preceding command starts the myVM virtual machine in the VMLab resource group.

Check the status using Get-AzureRmVM as before:

```
Get-AzureRmVM `
 -ResourceGroupName "VMLab" `
 -Name "myVM" `
 -Status
```

The preceding command will display the status of the myVM virtual machine.

The Restart VM command

To restart a VM, you can use the Restart-AzureRmVM command. Run the following command to restart the myVM virtual machine:

```
Restart-AzureRmVM -ResourceGroupName "VMLab" -Name "myVM"
```

The preceding command restarts the myVM virtual machine in the VMLab resource group.

Check the status using Get-AzureRmVM:

```
Get-AzureRmVM `
 -ResourceGroupName "VMLab" `
 -Name "myVM" `
 -Status
```

The preceding command will display the status of the myVM virtual machine.

The Remove VM command

There will be times when you need to decommission a VM. Doing so is performed with the Stop-AzureRmVM command. However, before deleting a VM, it should first be stopped. In this example, we'll stop the myVM virtual machine and then delete it.

To stop the VM, run the following command:

```
Stop-AzureRmVM -ResourceGroupName "VMLab" -Name "myVM" -Force
```

Once the VM is stopped, run the preceding Remove-AzureRmVM command to delete the VM:

```
Remove-AzureRmVM -ResourceGroupName "VMLab" -Name "myVM"
```

As was the case with the stop and start commands, only
the `ResourceGroupName` and `Name` switches need to be provided:

```
PS C:\Users\tmitchell> Remove-AzureRmVM -ResourceGroupName "VMLab" -Name "myVM"

Virtual machine removal operation
This cmdlet will remove the specified virtual machine. Do you want to continue?
[Y] Yes  [N] No  [S] Suspend  [?] Help (default is "Y"):
```

After a few minutes, run the following command to see whether the `myVM` virtual machine
has been deleted:

```
Get-AzureRmVM -status
```

If you've successfully deleted the VM, it should not be shown in the output of the preceding
command.

The only hassle with the `Remove-AzureRmVM` command is that it only removes the VM. It
does not clean up other resources that are attached to the VM, such as NICs or additional
disks. They need to be cleaned up manually, unless you opt to script their removal.

The Remove resource group command

The final command that I want to cover is the `Remove-`
`AzureRmResourceGroup` command. This command removes an entire resource group. I
personally use it quite regularly, since I'm always creating lab-and course-specific resource
groups. Once I'm done with the labs and courses, I just delete the resource groups so that
all resources inside the resource groups in their entirety are removed simultaneously. This
makes my life easier.

To remove the entire `VMLab` resource group, run the `Remove-`
`AzureRmResourceGroup` command. Don't worry; we'll be re-creating it later in this book:

```
Remove-AzureRmResourceGroup -Name "VMLab" -Force
```

Running this command tells Azure to delete the `VMLab` resource group and everything
inside it. The `Force` switch suppresses the **are you sure** prompts.

Although this command can sometimes take a while to complete, when it does complete,
the entire resource group is removed, along with everything inside of it.

After running the preceding command (and waiting a few minutes), run the following `Get-AzureRmResourceGroup` command to confirm that the `VMLab` resource group is gone:

```
Get-AzureRmResourceGroup -Name "VMLab"
```

 When operating in a production environment, you need to be careful when deleting resource groups. It's very easy to get into a lot of trouble if you aren't careful.

Your turn

Apply what you've learned in this chapter by completing the following project:

- **Project**: Common Commands
- **Project goal**: The goal of this project is to successfully deploy a VM and to practice stopping, starting, and removing it
- **Key commands**:
    - `New-AzureRmResourceGroup`
    - `Get-AzureRmResourceGroup`
    - `New-AzureRmVm`
    - `Get-AzureRmVM`
    - `Stop-AzureRmVM`
    - `Start-AzureRmVM`
    - `Remove-AzureRmVM`
    - `Remove-AzureRmResourceGroup`
- **General steps**:
    1. Create a resource group
    2. Deploy a VM with a default configuration
    3. Stop the VM
    4. Start the VM
    5. Delete the VM
    6. Delete the resource group and all its resources
- **Validation**: Ensure that the VM deploys, and that it stops and starts as expected
- **Reference info**: The *Basic Management Tasks* section

Summary

Congratulations! You've reached the end of this chapter. Here, we covered several basic skills.

You learned how to do the following:

- Install Azure PowerShell
- Deploy a VM
- Resize a VM with PowerShell
- Manage VM power states
- Perform basic VM management tasks (start, restart, stop, and delete)

Now that you know how to perform some basic tasks, we'll move on to the next chapter, where we will work with images.

Working with Images 2

Welcome to **Working with Images!** Now that you've (presumably) gone through and learned some of the Azure PowerShell basics in the previous chapter, we're going to take a look at some image-centric tasks and commands that you should know how to handle as part of your day-to-day operations.

In this chapter, we'll cover the following topics:

- Marketplace images
- Custom images

By the end of this chapter, you should know how to deploy virtual machines from the existing images that are available on the Azure Marketplace and from custom-created images. You will even get the opportunity to practice what you've learned by workign through a hands-on exercise at the end of the chapter.

Working with Marketplace Images

Although a virtual machine can be deployed in Azure with default options, the Azure marketplace offers numerous virtual machine images that can be used to create a new virtual machine.

If you are following along, you previously deployed a virtual machine, called MyVM, using the default Windows Server 2016-Datacenter image (because you didn't choose a specific image to use). However, here, I'm going to explain how to use PowerShell to search the marketplace for other Windows images and how to deploy a new virtual machine in Azure using one of those images.

Before performing any exercises in this section, run the following command to recreate the VMLab resource group if you've deleted it:

```
New-AzureRmResourceGroup -ResourceGroupName "VMLab" -Location "EastUS"
```

The preceding command should generate the output you see here:

```
PS C:\Users\tmitchell> New-AzureRmResourceGroup -ResourceGroupName "VMLab" -Location "EastUS"

ResourceGroupName : VMLab
Location          : eastus
ProvisioningState : Succeeded
Tags              :
ResourceId        : /subscriptions/0aec89a4-d5f8-4343-b43b-1ec899719dfe/resourceGroups/VMLab
```

To confirm that your new VMLab resource group exists, run the following command:

```
Get-AzureRmResourceGroup
```

Ensure that the new VMLab resource group is listed.

Key PowerShell commands

The process of deploying a virtual machine using a specific image includes finding a publisher, finding an offer from that publisher, and then locating a SKU for the image to use.

To work through this process, you need to run three different PowerShell commands:

- `Get-AzureRmVMImagePublisher`: This command returns a list of image publishers.
- `Get-AzureRmVMImageOffer`: This command returns a list of image offers from a specific publisher.
- `Get-AzureRmVMImageSku`: This command will filter on the publisher and offer name to return a list of available image names.

The process seems, on the surface, a bit unwieldy, but it's not terribly difficult. Once you've done it a few times, it's really does become second nature:

1. To track down an image to deploy from, launch a PowerShell session, connect to the Azure tenant, and use the following commands, starting with the `Get-AzureRmVMImagePublisher` command:

    Get-AzureRmVMImagePublisher -Location "EastUS"

    As you can see in the following screenshot, the preceding command returns a list of publishers available in the `EastUS` location. If you are following along, make sure **MicrosoftWindowsServer** is listed, since this is the publisher that provides Windows OS images on the marketplace. The following screenshot shows all publishers in the EastUS location:

2. After ensuring that **MicrosoftWindowsServer** is listed, run the `Get-AzureRmVMImageOffer` command to see what image offers are available in the `EastUS` location from the **MicrosoftWindowsServer** publisher:

    Get-AzureRmVMImageOffer `
    -Location "EastUS" `
    -PublisherName MicrosoftWindowsServer

As of this writing, there are three **MicrosoftWindowsServer** offers available in EastUS. To deploy a Windows virtual machine, you'll want to ensure **WindowsServer** is one of the choices available. The following screenshot shows the available image offers from the **MicrosoftWindowsServer** publisher in the EastUS location:

3. Track down available image names within the **WindowsServer** offer, using the `Get-AzureRmVMImageSKU` command:

```
Get-AzureRmVMImageSku `
  -Location "EastUS" `
  -PublisherName "MicrosoftWindowsServer" `
  -Offer "WindowsServer"
```

Running the preceding command returns quite a few options. Keep in mind that the list you see (if you are following along) is filtered, based on the specified Publisher and Image Offer. For this exercise, you'll want to ultimately choose the **2016-Datacenter** option—since that is the OS we are going to deploy in this exercise. In the following screenshot, you can see the many different SKUs that are available through the **WindowsServer** offer from the **MicrosoftWindowsServer** publisher:

```
PS C:\Users\tmitchell> Get-AzureRmVMImageSku -Location "EastUS" -PublisherName "MicrosoftWindowsServer" -Offer "WindowsServer"

Skus                                     Offer          PublisherName          Location Id
----                                     -----          -------------          -------- --
2008-R2-SP1                              WindowsServer  MicrosoftWindowsServer eastus   /Subscriptions/4eacb230-3e94-4bec-9cb8-2a5be79fb60e/Providers/...
2008-R2-SP1-smalldisk                    WindowsServer  MicrosoftWindowsServer eastus   /Subscriptions/4eacb230-3e94-4bec-9cb8-2a5be79fb60e/Providers/...
2012-Datacenter                          WindowsServer  MicrosoftWindowsServer eastus   /Subscriptions/4eacb230-3e94-4bec-9cb8-2a5be79fb60e/Providers/...
2012-Datacenter-smalldisk                WindowsServer  MicrosoftWindowsServer eastus   /Subscriptions/4eacb230-3e94-4bec-9cb8-2a5be79fb60e/Providers/...
2012-R2-Datacenter                       WindowsServer  MicrosoftWindowsServer eastus   /Subscriptions/4eacb230-3e94-4bec-9cb8-2a5be79fb60e/Providers/...
2012-R2-Datacenter-smalldisk             WindowsServer  MicrosoftWindowsServer eastus   /Subscriptions/4eacb230-3e94-4bec-9cb8-2a5be79fb60e/Providers/...
2016-Datacenter                          WindowsServer  MicrosoftWindowsServer eastus   /Subscriptions/4eacb230-3e94-4bec-9cb8-2a5be79fb60e/Providers/...
2016-Datacenter-Server-Core              WindowsServer  MicrosoftWindowsServer eastus   /Subscriptions/4eacb230-3e94-4bec-9cb8-2a5be79fb60e/Providers/...
2016-Datacenter-Server-Core-smalldisk    WindowsServer  MicrosoftWindowsServer eastus   /Subscriptions/4eacb230-3e94-4bec-9cb8-2a5be79fb60e/Providers/...
2016-Datacenter-smalldisk                WindowsServer  MicrosoftWindowsServer eastus   /Subscriptions/4eacb230-3e94-4bec-9cb8-2a5be79fb60e/Providers/...
2016-Datacenter-with-Containers          WindowsServer  MicrosoftWindowsServer eastus   /Subscriptions/4eacb230-3e94-4bec-9cb8-2a5be79fb60e/Providers/...
2016-Datacenter-with-RDSH                WindowsServer  MicrosoftWindowsServer eastus   /Subscriptions/4eacb230-3e94-4bec-9cb8-2a5be79fb60e/Providers/...
2016-Nano-Server                         WindowsServer  MicrosoftWindowsServer eastus   /Subscriptions/4eacb230-3e94-4bec-9cb8-2a5be79fb60e/Providers/...
```

Now that you know which publisher you are using, which offer you will need, and which image you are going to deploy from, you can deploy a virtual machine using your chosen image.

Provisioning a new virtual machine from a specific image

In the previous section, we decided we would use the **2016-Datacenter** image for a new virtual machine. In this section, I am going to explain how to deploy a virtual machine based on the **2016-Datacenter** image, within the **WindowsServer** offer, from the **MicrosoftWindowsServer** publisher.

To deploy the new virtual machine, which we are going to call myVM2, you need to first capture some credentials to use as the local admin for the new virtual machine. To specify the local admin credentials for the new virtual machine, run the following command:

```
$cred = Get-Credential
```

To deploy a new virtual machine (called myVM2), using the preceding information, run the New-AzureRmVm command in a PowerShell session that's been connected to your Azure tenant:

```
New-AzureRmVm `
 -ResourceGroupName "VMLab" `
 -Name "myVM2" `
 -Location "EastUS" `
 -VirtualNetworkName "myVnet" `
 -SubnetName "mySubnet" `
 -SecurityGroupName "myNSG" `
 -PublicIpAddressName "myPublicIpAddress2" `
 -ImageName "MicrosoftWindowsServer:WindowsServer:2016-Datacenter:latest" `
 -Credential $cred `
 -AsJob
```

You might notice that the preceding command looks very similar to the original command that we used earlier in this book to provision the initial virtual machine (myVM) using the default image. However, if you look closely at this new iteration, you'll see two new switches added to it. You'll see ImageName specified, as well as AsJob. These are two new switches that were not included when the MyVM virtual machine was first deployed.

The ImageName switch specifies the value returned by the Get-AzureRmVMImageSku command in the previous section. This is the switch that tells Azure what specific image to deploy the new virtual machine from.

The AsJob switch creates the virtual machine as a background task and returns control of the PowerShell prompt to you, so you can continue working without needing to wait for the previous command to complete.

Since this command is deploying a virtual machine, it can take a while to complete. After a few minutes (usually 15 minutes or so), the new myVM2 virtual machine will be deployed:

```
PS C:\Users\tmitchell> New-AzureRmVm `
>>     -ResourceGroupName "VMLab" `
>>     -Name "myVM2" `
>>     -Location "EastUS" `
>>     -VirtualNetworkName "myVnet" `
>>     -SubnetName "mySubnet" `
>>     -SecurityGroupName "myNSG" `
>>     -PublicIpAddressName "myPublicIpAddress2" `
>>     -ImageName "MicrosoftWindowsServer:WindowsServer:2016-Datacenter:latest" `
>>     -Credential $cred `
>>     -AsJob

Id    Name            PSJobTypeName     State      HasMoreData    Location      Command
--    ----            -------------     -----      -----------    --------      -------
1     Long Running... AzureLongRun...   Running    True           localhost     New-AzureRmVM
```

Before continuing, you can run the following Get-AzureRmVm command and confirm that the myVM2 virtual machine is deployed and running:

```
Get-AzureRmVm -ResourceGroupName VMLab -Name MyVM2 -status
```

Assuming you did everything right, you will be able to see the following output, indicating that the new myVM2 virtual machine has been deployed and is running:

```
ResourceGroupName : VMLab
Name              : myVM2
Disks[0]          :
  Name            : myVM2_OsDisk_1_f0ff24e333764ecbbe905dcd7a7da844
  Statuses[0]     :
    Code          : ProvisioningState/succeeded
    Level         : Info
    DisplayStatus : Provisioning succeeded
    Time          : 6/6/2018 10:18:56 AM
Statuses[0]       :
  Code            : ProvisioningState/creating
  Level           : Info
  DisplayStatus   : Creating
Statuses[1]       :
  Code            : PowerState/running
  Level           : Info
  DisplayStatus   : VM running
```

Using custom images

So far, you've learned how to create a virtual machine, using the default image. You've also learned how to deploy a virtual machine, using a specific image from the marketplace.

Sometimes, though, a default or marketplace image just isn't sufficient for a virtual machine's deployment. An example of this in the real world would be a case where several virtual machines with a particular application installed are needed. Another example would be a case where a **gold image** server image is maintained so that when a virtual machine is deployed from it, the server that gets deployed is already fully patched, negating the need to spend hours patching it up to date.

Enter Custom Images.

Custom images are essentially the same as images available on the marketplace. However, custom images are created by you. By using custom images, you can deploy preconfigured servers, saving yourself hours of post-deployment configuration.

In this section, we will create a custom image of an Azure virtual machine and use it to deploy a customized virtual machine.

You will learn how to do the following:

- Sysprep and generalize a virtual machine
- Create a custom image from an existing virtual machine
- Create a new virtual machine from a custom image
- List all the images in an Azure subscription
- Delete an image

 The skills you learn are skills that many other IT professionals do not possess. As such, learning these skills puts you ahead of many of your peers.

Before you begin

Throughout the rest of this exercise, I'm going to walk you through the steps required to take an existing virtual machine, create a custom image from it, and then use that image to deploy a new customized virtual machine based on the image.

To follow along with this exercise, you need to have an existing Windows 2016 virtual machine, called myVM2, in Azure to work with. It should be deployed to a resource group called VMLab, per the previous section.

Preparing a virtual machine

The first step in deploying a virtual machine based on a custom image is to prepare the source virtual machine. Creating an image from a source virtual machine requires the source virtual machine to be *generalized* and *deallocated*. Once this has been completed, the source virtual machine needs to be marked as generalized in Azure. Only after these tasks have been completed can an image be made from the virtual machine.

Using sysprep

Sysprep is the tool that's used to generalize the source virtual machine. It is a Windows utility that essentially removes all account information from a machine. What this tool does is remove security information, such as the SID/GUID, from a virtual machine and then it prepares the computer for a first-time boot— much like a new laptop would behave upon the initial boot.

Removing all security information from a virtual machine allows an image of it to be taken and used over and over without duplicate SIDs/GUIDs causing issues related to having multiple identical computers on the network.

To begin the process of preparing the myVM2 virtual machine to be used as an image, perform the following steps:

1. Log in to the virtual machine using RDP and launch the Command Prompt as an administrator. Get the public IP for the virtual machine so you can RDP to it by running the following command:

```
Get-AzureRmPublicIpAddress `
  -Name myPublicIPaddress2 `
  -ResourceGroupName VMLab | Select IPAddress
```

2. Once you've logged into myVM2, launch the command prompt as an admin and change to the %windir%\system32\sysprep directory and run sysprep.exe:

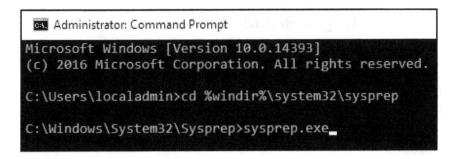

3. From the **System Preparation Tool** dialog box, choose **Enter System Out-of-Box Experience (OOBE)** and make sure that the **Generalize** checkbox is checked. In **Shutdown Options**, select **Shutdown** and then click **OK**:

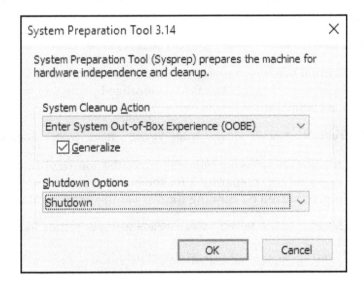

4. Clicking **OK** launches the Sysprep process. When Sysprep completes, the virtual machine is automatically shut down.

 DO NOT RESTART THE VIRTUAL MACHINE!

Deallocating and generalizing

Before creating an image from the source virtual machine, the virtual machine must first be deallocated and marked as *generalized* in Azure:

1. Confirm the myVM2 virtual machine has been shut down by running the Get-AzureRmVm command:

   Get-AzureRmVm –Name MyVM2 –ResourceGroupName VMLab –status

2. Stop and deallocate the virtual machine by running the following command:

   Stop-AzureRmVm –ResourceGroupName VMLab –Name myVM2 –Force

3. Run the Get-AzureRmVm command to be sure the virtual machine is stopped and deallocated:

   Get-AzureRmVm –Name MyVM2 –ResourceGroupName VMLab –status

4. Once the virtual machine has stopped and shows **deallocated** when you run Get-AzureRmVm, set its status to **generalized** using the Set-AzureRmVm command:

   Set-AzureRmVM –ResourceGroupName VMLab –Name myVM2 –Generalized

5. Running the preceding command deallocates the source virtual machine and marks it as *generalized*, preparing it for the imaging process. Confirm that the machine is generalized by running the Get-AzureRmVm command:

   Get-AzureRmVm –Name MyVM2 –ResourceGroupName VMLab –status

You should see *VM generalized* as one of the statuses listed.

Creating an image

With the source virtual machine (myVM2) generalized and deallocated, it can now be used to generate an image. Creating an image requires the use of two different PowerShell commands: New-AzureRmImageConfig and New-AzureRmImage.

To create an image from myVM2, three things need to happen. First, the myVM2 virtual machine config needs to be loaded into a variable. Second, the image configuration needs to be created from myVM2. And third, the actual image needs to be created.

Follow these instructions to complete the necessary steps.

Retrieving the source VM

Run the following command to retrieve the source myVM2 info and store it in a variable:

```
$vm = Get-AzureRmVM -Name myVM2 -ResourceGroupName VMLab
```

This command will not generate any feedback on the screen, since all it's doing is loading info into a variable.

Creating an image configuration

Run the New-AzureRmImageConfig command to create an image configuration that will be used to create the eventual image:

```
$image = New-AzureRmImageConfig `
-Location EastUS `
-SourceVirtualMachineId $vm.ID
```

Creating an image

The last step in the image creation is the actual creation of the image from the image configuration. Run the New-AzureRmImage command to create the actual image:

```
New-AzureRmImage `
-Image $image `
-ImageName myImage `
-ResourceGroupName VMLab
```

Upon completion of the preceding steps, you are left with a new image, called myImage. The following screenshot shows the new image that was successfully created:

```
ResourceGroupName   : VMLab
SourceVirtualMachine : Microsoft.Azure.Management.Compute.Models.SubResource
StorageProfile      : Microsoft.Azure.Management.Compute.Models.ImageStorageProfile
ProvisioningState   : Succeeded
Id                  : /subscriptions/0aec89a4-d5f8-4343-b43b-1ec899719dfe/resourceGroups/VMLab/providers/Microsoft.Compute/images/myImage
Name                : myImage
Type                : Microsoft.Compute/images
Location            : eastus
Tags                : {}
```

This image, based on the myVM2 virtual machine, can be used to deploy additional virtual machines that will be configured identically to myVM2.

Creating a VM from an image

Once an image has been created, it can be used to provision additional virtual machines. Creating a new virtual machine in Azure from a custom image isn't terribly different than creating a virtual machine using a typical Marketplace image.

When you deploy an Azure virtual machine from a Marketplace image, you must provide information about the image publisher, the offer, the SKU, and the version.

Using a basic set of parameters (switches) for the New-AzureRmVm command allows you to just provide the name of the custom image (if it is in the same resource group as the virtual machine you are deploying).

The following **New-AzureRmVm** command will provision a new virtual machine in Azure, called myVM3, using the image called myImage. Run the command to create a new virtual machine, called MyVM3:

```
New-AzureRmVm `
-ResourceGroupName "VMLab" `
-Name "myVM3" `
-ImageName "myImage" `
-Location "EastUS" `
-VirtualNetworkName "myVnet" `
-SubnetName "mySubnet" `
-SecurityGroupName "myNSG" `
-PublicIpAddressName "myPublicIP3"
```

Because you didn't create local admin credentials before running the preceding command, you will be prompted to create local admin credentials. Once you supply them, the new myVM3 virtual machine will be provisioned. Running the **New-AzureRmVm** command should produce output similar to what you see here:

```
Creating Azure resources
  32% -
  [ooooooooooooooooooooooooooooooooooooooooooooo                                                           ]

  Creating virtualMachines/myVM3.


ResourceGroupName      : VMLab
SourceVirtualMachine   : Microsoft.Azure.Management.Compute.Models.SubResource
StorageProfile         : Microsoft.Azure.Management.Compute.Models.ImageStorageProfile
ProvisioningState      : Succeeded
Id                     : /subscriptions/0aec89a4-d5f8-4343-b43b-1ec899719dfe/resourceGroups/VMLab/providers/Microsoft.Compute/images/myImage
Name                   : myImage
Type                   : Microsoft.Compute/images
Location               : eastus
Tags                   : {}


PS C:\Users\tmitchell> New-AzureRmVm `
>>      -ResourceGroupName "VMLab" `
>>      -Name "myVM3" `
>>      -ImageName "myImage" `
>>      -Location "EastUS" `
>>      -VirtualNetworkName "myVnet" `
>>      -SubnetName "mySubnet" `
>>      -SecurityGroupName "myNSG" `
>>      -PublicIpAddressName "myPublicIP3"

cmdlet New-AzureRmVM at command pipeline position 1
Supply values for the following parameters:
Credential
WARNING: New-AzureRmVM: A property of the output of this cmdlet will change in an upcoming breaking change release. The StorageAccountType property
for a DataDisk will return Standard_LRS and Premium_LRS
```

Once the preceding command completes, run the following command to retrieve the public IP for myVM3 and use it to RDP into the new virtual machine and confirm it functions as expected:

```
Get-AzureRmPublicIpAddress `
-Name myPublicIP3 `
-ResourceGroupName VMLab | Select IPAddress
```

Once you've confirmed the new virtual machine works as expected, continue with the next exercise.

Managing images

Deploying a new virtual machine from an image is all well and good. However, it helps to know how to perform some basic image-management tasks as well. You can use the following instructions to perform some common image-management tasks via PowerShell.

Listing images by name

The following command enables you to list all available images by name:

```
Find-AzureRmResource -ResourceType Microsoft.Compute/images
```

Deleting an Image

The following command deletes the myImage image from the VMLab resource group:

```
Remove-AzureRmImage -ImageName myImage -ResourceGroupName VMLab
```

Don't worry, deleting the image won't break the virtual machine that you deployed from it. The image just won't be available to create any more VMs:

```
PS C:\Users\tmitchell> Remove-AzureRmImage `
>>      -ImageName myImage `
>>      -ResourceGroupName VMLab

Remove-AzureRmImage operation
This cmdlet will remove the specified resource.  Do you want to continue?
[Y] Yes  [N] No  [S] Suspend  [?] Help (default is "Y"):
```

Congratulations! You've now learned how to create a disk image from an existing virtual machine and then use that image to deploy a new virtual machine—all with PowerShell!

Your turn

- **Project**: Custom disk images
- **Project goal**: To successfully provision a virtual machine, based on a disk image taken from an existing virtual machine
- **Key commands**:
    - New-AzureRmResourceGroup
    - Get-AzureRmPublicIpAddress
    - Get-AzureRmVm
    - Stop-AzureRmVm
    - Set-AzureRmVM
    - New-AzureRmImageConfig
    - New-AzureRmImage
    - Get-Credential
    - New-AzureRmVm
    - Remove-AzureRmResourceGroup

- **General steps:**
  1. Create a resource group
  2. Deploy a virtual machine with a default configuration
  3. Take an image of the OS disk of the virtual machine
  4. Delete the virtual machine
  5. Deploy a second virtual machine from the image
  6. Delete the resource group and all resources
- **Validation**: Ensure that the new virtual machine deploys successfully by logging into it after deploying it from the disk image
- **Reference info**: Using custom images

Summary

Good job! You've now completed this chapter. In this chapter, we covered Marketplace Images and Custom Images.

You learned how to deploy virtual machines from images in the Marketplace and also how to deploy virtual machines with custom images.

It's time to move on to the next chapter, where we will cover virtual disks.

Working with Disks 3

Welcome to *Working with Disks!* In the course of your day-to-day operations, you'll often find that you need to perform tasks such as snapshotting or encryption. In this chapter, we will cover the following topics:

- Azure data disks
- Snapshotting an Azure virtual machine
- Creating
- VMs from Snapshots
- Encrypting virtual machine disks

This chapter also includes hands-on exercises that allow you to practice your skills with data disks, snapshots, and encryption.

When all is said and done, you'll know how to create and attach data disks, snapshot them, encrypt them, and even deploy new VMs from them.

Using Azure data disks

Azure virtual machines use disks to store the operating systems, applications, and data. Choosing an appropriate disk size and configuration is crucial when creating a virtual machine. You want to make sure that you size and configure your disks to match whatever workload the server will be handling. The following exercises cover deploying virtual machine data disks and managing them.

The next few exercises will teach you about:

- The difference between OS disks and temporary disks
- What Data Disks are
- The difference between standard disks and premium disks

- Disk performance
- How to create data disks
- How to attach a data disk to a virtual machine
- How to prepare a data disk for use

When you finish these exercises, you will have a solid understanding of the different types of Azure disks, how to create them via PowerShell, and how to manage them via PowerShell.

Default Azure disks

When an Azure virtual machine is created, two disks are automatically attached to the virtual machine. They include the operating system disk and a temporary disk.

Operating system disk

Operating system disks, which host the virtual machine's OS, can be up to 4 terabytes. The OS disk is assigned a drive letter of `C:` by default, and its disk-caching configuration is optimized for OS performance. It is not recommended to use the OS disk to host data or applications. Instead, for applications and data, use a data disk, which is detailed later in this article.

Temporary disk

Temporary disks use a solid-state drive that is located on the same Azure host as the virtual machine. This temporary storage is typically used to save the system paging file, but can be used to store other data that you can afford to lose. There is no extra storage associated with this temporary storage.

Temporary disks are high performance, and can be used for operations such as temporary data processing. However, if the virtual machine is moved to a new host, then the data stored on the temporary disk will be removed. The size of a temporary disk is generally determined by the virtual machine size, and they are typically assigned a drive letter of `D:` by default.

Temporary disk sizes

The sizes of temporary disks, as of the time of writing, are summarized here:

- **General purpose**:
    - A, B, and D Series VM
    - 1,600 MB
- **Compute-optimized**:
    - F Series VM
    - 576 MB
- **Memory-optimized**:
    - D, E, G, and M Series VM
    - 6,144 MB
- **Storage-optimized**:
    - L Series VM
    - 5,630 MB
- **GPU**:
    - N Series VM
    - 1,440 MB
- **High-performance**:
    - A and H Series VM
    - 2,000 MB

Azure data disks

Data disks are recommended when durable and responsive data storage is required. Each data disk has a maximum size of 4 TB. However, multiple data disks can be attached to a virtual machine. When installing applications and storing data, data disks should be used.

The size of the virtual machine determines how many data disks can be attached to it. The number of virtual CPUs is typically what drives this.

Maximum data disks per VM

Although the absolute maximum number of data disks that can be attached to a virtual machine is 64, the type and size of a virtual machine dictates the maximum number of data disks that can be attached, as summarized here:

- **General-purpose**:
    - A, B, and D series VM
    - 2-64 data disks
- **Compute-optimized**:
    - F series VM
    - 4-64 data disks
- **Memory-optimized**:
    - D, E, G, and M Series VM
    - 4-64 data disks
- **Storage-optimized**:
    - L series VM
    - 16-64 data disks
- **GPU**:
    - N series VM
    - 12-64 data disks
- **High-performance**:
    - A and H series VM
    - 32-64 data disks

VM disk types

Azure provides two types of disk; these include standard disks and premium disks. Standard disks are typically lower-performance and are used for general-purpose storage. Premium disks are higher-performance, and are used when higher IO is required.

Standard disk

Standard storage is backed by magnetic HDD technology and delivers cost-effective storage while still providing decent performance. Standard disks are ideal for cost-effective development environments.

Premium disk

Premium disks are backed by **solid-state (SSD) technology**. Low-latency disks, such as SSD, offer high-performance storage. Premium disks are a good choice for production-virtual machines and VMs that require high IO. Premium storage supports DS series, DSv2 series, GS series, and FS series virtual machines, and comes in five types: P10, P20, P30, P40, and P50.

Premium disk performance

The size of the disk determines the disk type. When you provision a premium disk, the size is rounded up to the next type. For example, if a disk being provisioned is below 128GB, the disk type is P10. However, a disk of 200GB would be P20. The following table highlights the differences:

Type	P4	P6	P10	P20	P30	P40	P50
Size	32 GB	64 GB	128 GB	512 GB	1 TB	2 TB	4 TB
Max IOPs	120	240	500	2,300	5,000	7,500	7,500
Throughput (MB/s)	25	50	100	150	200	250	250

Although this table identifies the maximum number of IOPS per disk, stripping multiple data disks can achieve even higher performance.

Creating and attaching disks

Creating a disk and attaching it to a virtual machine requires four steps. The first step is to create the initial disk configuration. Once the configuration is created, the actual data disk resource is created. After creating the configuration and the actual data disk, the data disk is added to the virtual machine configuration. Lastly, the virtual machine configuration is updated to include the new disk.

The following exercises demonstrate how to create a new data disk and how to add the data disk to the myVM3 virtual machine. Follow these instructions to create a new data disk and to attach the data disk to the myVM3 virtual machine.

Creating the data disk configuration

Create the initial configuration with the New-AzureRmDiskConfig command. The following command configures a disk that is 128 GB in size. Copy and paste it into your PowerShell session and run it. The new disk configuration is stored in a variable called $diskConfig so it can be more easily referenced in later commands:

```
$diskConfig = New-AzureRmDiskConfig `
 -Location "EastUS" `
 -CreateOption Empty `
 -DiskSizeGB 128
```

The preceding command generates no feedback on the screen.

Creating the data disk

With the data disk configuration created, create the actual data disk with the New-AzureRmDisk command:

```
$dataDisk = New-AzureRmDisk `
 -ResourceGroupName "VMLab" `
 -DiskName "DataDisk" `
 -Disk $diskConfig
```

This command takes a few minutes to complete and produces no feedback on screen. New-AzureRmDisk creates an actual data disk resource that's based on the disk configuration that you created in the first step.

Adding the data disk to the virtual machine

With the data disk created, get the virtual machine that you are adding the data disk to by running the following Get-AzureRmVM command:

```
$vm = Get-AzureRmVM -ResourceGroupName "VMLab" -Name "myVM3"
```

The preceding command retrieves the virtual machine configuration for the myVM3 virtual machine and loads it into a variable called $vm. You can add the data disk to the virtual machine configuration using the Add-AzureRmVMDataDisk command:

```
$vm = Add-AzureRmVMDataDisk `
 -VM $vm `
 -Name "DataDisk" `
 -CreateOption Attach `
 -ManagedDiskId $dataDisk.Id `
 -Lun 1
```

This command doesn't actually update the virtual machine yet; it adds the new data disk to the virtual machine configuration. The next step will take that updated configuration and apply it to the actual virtual machine.

Updating the virtual machine

With the data disk configuration added to the virtual machine configuration (using the preceding command), the virtual machine can be updated using the Update-AzureRmVM command:

```
Update-AzureRmVm -ResourceGroupName "VMLab" -VM $vm
```

The preceding command adds the actual data disk to the virtual machine so that the OS of the virtual machine can see it. This can take a minute or two to complete:

```
PS C:\Users\tmitchell> Update-AzureRmVm -ResourceGroupName "VMLab" -VM $vm

RequestId IsSuccessStatusCode StatusCode ReasonPhrase
--------- ------------------- ---------- ------------
                         True         OK OK
```

Preparing data disks

After attaching a data disk to a virtual machine, the disk must be configured within the operating system on the virtual machine itself. The disk must be initialized, and a partition created. The partition must then be formatted (just like any other physical disk would be).

The following exercise demonstrates how to manually configure a data disk added to a virtual machine.

Manually configuring an attached disk

To manually configure the newly attached data disk on myVM3, simply create an RDP connection to the virtual machine and open PowerShell on it.

Run the following command in the PowerShell session and hit *Enter*:

```
Get-Disk | Where partitionstyle -eq 'raw' | `
  Initialize-Disk -PartitionStyle MBR -PassThru | `
  New-Partition -AssignDriveLetter -UseMaximumSize | `
  Format-Volume -FileSystem NTFS `
  -NewFileSystemLabel "DataDisk" `
  -Confirm:$false
```

The preceding command is one long command. It retrieves the raw disk, using the `Get-Disk` command. From there, it pipes that information to the `Initialize-Disk` command so that the disk can be initialized within the operating system:

```
Windows PowerShell
Copyright (C) 2016 Microsoft Corporation. All rights reserved.

PS C:\Users\localadmin> Get-Disk | Where partitionstyle -eq 'raw' | `
>> Initialize-Disk -PartitionStyle MBR -PassThru | `
>> New-Partition -AssignDriveLetter -UseMaximumSize | `
>> Format-Volume -FileSystem NTFS -NewFileSystemLabel "DataDisk" -Confirm:$false

DriveLetter FileSystemLabel FileSystem DriveType HealthStatus OperationalStatus SizeRemaining    Size
----------- --------------- ---------- --------- ------------ ----------------- -------------    ----
F           DataDisk        NTFS       Fixed     Healthy      OK                127.89 GB    128 GB

PS C:\Users\localadmin> _
```

Once the disk is initialized, the `New-Partition` command creates a new partition that equals the size of the disk. Lastly, the `Format-Volume` command formats the new volume so that it can be accessed by the operating system:

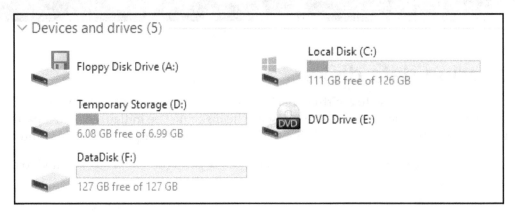

Your turn

- **Project**: Data disks
- **Project goal**: The goal of this project is to successfully provision a data disk, connect it to a virtual machine, and make it available to the operating system on the virtual machine
- **Key commands**:
    - New-AzureRmResourceGroup
    - New-AzureRmVm
    - New-AzureRmDiskConfig
    - New-AzureRmDisk
    - Get-AzureRmVM
    - Add-AzureRmVMDataDisk
    - Update-AzureRmVm
    - Get-Disk
    - Initialize-Disk
    - New-Partition
    - Format-Volume
    - Remove-AzureRmResourceGroup
- **General steps**:
    1. Create a resource group
    2. Deploy a virtual machine with a default configuration
    3. Create a data disk
    4. Attach the data disk to the virtual machine
    5. Initialize and format the attached data disk
- **Validation**: Log into the virtual machine and confirm that the new data disk is available to the operating system and is writeable by creating a text file on it
- **Reference info**: The *Using Azure data disks* section

Snapshotting an Azure VM disk

Another way to create custom virtual machines is to deploy them from an existing snapshot from another virtual machine. To do this, you first need to create a snapshot of an existing virtual machine.

The following exercises show you how to create the snapshot configuration for an existing virtual machine and how to take a snapshot of the disk using the `New-AzureRmSnapshot` cmdlet.

Setting snapshot parameters

Before snapshotting a virtual machine, a few parameters/variables need to be set so they can be more easily referenced later. We need to set the resource group name, the location where the source virtual machine resides, and a name for the snapshot.

Run the following commands to set the parameters to create a snapshot of myVM3:

```
$resourceGroupName = 'VMLab'
$location = 'EastUS'
$vmName = 'myVM3'
$snapshotName = 'mySnapshot'
```

The preceding commands generate no output:

```
PS C:\Users\tmitchell> $resourceGroupName = 'VMLab'
PS C:\Users\tmitchell> $location = 'EastUS'
PS C:\Users\tmitchell> $vmName = 'myVM3'
PS C:\Users\tmitchell> $snapshotName = 'mySnapshot'
```

Getting the VM

With the command variables set, you can then retrieve the configuration of the myVM3 virtual machine and store it in a variable, called $vm. Once the existing configuration of myVM3 is stored in the variable, it will be used to create the snapshot.

Run the following Get-AzureRmVm command to retrieve the myVM3 virtual machine configuration and store it in the variable:

```
$vm = Get-AzureRmVm `
 -ResourceGroupName $resourceGroupName `
 -Name $vmName
```

This command takes a few moments to run sometimes.

Creating the snapshot configuration

Once the parameters have been set and the source virtual machine configuration has been retrieved, we can create the snapshot configuration. To create the snapshot configuration, run the `New-AzureRmSnapshotConfig` command:

```
$snapshot = New-AzureRmSnapshotConfig `
 -SourceUri $vm.StorageProfile.OsDisk.ManagedDisk.Id `
 -Location $location `
 -CreateOption copy
```

This command provides no feedback on the screen.

Taking the snapshot

After creating the snapshot configuration, the actual snapshot of the source virtual machine (myVM3) can be taken, using the `New-AzureRmSnapshot` command. To create the actual snapshot, run the following command:

```
New-AzureRmSnapshot `
 -Snapshot $snapshot `
 -SnapshotName $snapshotName `
 -ResourceGroupName $resourceGroupName
```

The preceding command creates the snapshot, based on the snapshot configuration that you previously stored in the `$snapshot` variable. By specifying the VMLab resource group, via the `$resourceGroupName` variable that you set earlier, the snapshot is stored in the VMLab resource group:

```
ResourceGroupName  : VMLab
ManagedBy          :
Sku                : Microsoft.Azure.Management.Compute.Models.SnapshotSku
TimeCreated        : 6/6/2018 7:48:07 AM
OsType             : Windows
CreationData       : Microsoft.Azure.Management.Compute.Models.CreationData
DiskSizeGB         : 127
EncryptionSettings :
ProvisioningState  : Succeeded
Id                 : /subscriptions/0aec89a4-d5f8-4343-b43b-1ec899719dfe/resourceGroups/VMLab/providers/Microsoft.Compute/snapshots/mySnapshot
Name               : mySnapshot
Type               : Microsoft.Compute/snapshots
Location           : eastus
Tags               : {}
```

Once the snapshot is completed, you can create a virtual machine from it by creating a managed disk from the snapshot and then attaching the new managed disk as the OS disk. You will create a new virtual machine from this snapshot in the next section.

Creating VMs from Snapshots

Once a snapshot has been taken of an existing virtual machine, the snapshot can be used to create a new virtual machine. In this section, we will cover the deployment of a new virtual machine, using a snapshot as the OS disk for the new virtual machine.

The process of deploying a new virtual machine, using a snapshot, includes a few different steps. The first step is to load up required variables with information about the snapshot and the disk config for the new virtual machine.

Once the variables are loaded, the configuration for the new virtual machine needs to be initialized. This process includes setting the virtual machine size, deploying a public IP address, provisioning an NIC, and telling the process which virtual network to deploy the virtual machine to.

After initializing the configuration for the new virtual machine, the virtual machine can be created.

Loading Variables

Loading the necessary variables requires three commands. The first command loads the existing snapshot that was created into a variable, called $snapshot. The snapshot info needs to be loaded into a variable so that it can be more easily referenced in commands used later in the process.

Load the snapshot config for the mySnaphsot snapshot into a variable by running the following command:

```
$snapshot = Get-AzureRmSnapshot `
 -ResourceGroupName 'VMLab' `
 -SnapshotName 'mySnapshot'
```

Once the snapshot config is loaded into a variable, you need to create a new disk configuration and load that into a separate variable so that it, too, can be referenced more easily:

```
$diskConfig = New-AzureRmDiskConfig `
 -Location $snapshot.Location `
 -SourceResourceId $snapshot.Id `
 -CreateOption Copy
```

After loading the new disk configuration into a variable, using the preceding command, you need to create a new OS disk resource based on the configuration you just loaded. To create the OS disk resource based on the preceding configuration, run the NewAzureRmDisk command:

```
$disk = New-AzureRmDisk `
 -Disk $diskConfig `
 -ResourceGroupName VMLab `
 -DiskName myOSDisk
```

None of these three commands is going to produce any feedback on the screen; however, they are loading up the snapshot configuration, creating a disk configuration based on the snapshot that was taken, and provisioning a new OS disk from the snapshot.

Initializing the virtual machine configuration

Initializing the new virtual machine that will be deployed from the snapshot requires quite a few steps. First, a configuration for the new virtual machine needs to be loaded into a variable so it can be modified. Next, the OS disk needs to be appended to the virtual machine configuration that's stored in the variable. After that, the network info needs to be added to the virtual machine configuration. This info includes adding a public IP, setting the virtual network that the virtual machine will attach to, and setting the NIC and subnet for the new virtual machine. This info is all set up by loading it into variables.

Run the following commands to set up the configuration for the new virtual machine being deployed from the image:

```
$vm = New-AzureRmVMConfig -VMName 'myVM4' -VMSize 'Standard_A2_V2'
```

Use the Managed Disk Resource ID to attach it to the virtual machine:

```
$vm = Set-AzureRmVMOSDisk `
 -VM $vm `
 -ManagedDiskId $disk.Id `
 -CreateOption Attach `
 -Windows
```

Run the following command to create a public IP for the new virtual machine (myVM4):

```
$pip = New-AzureRmPublicIpAddress `
 -Name 'myPublicIP4' `
 -ResourceGroupName 'VMLab' `
 -Location $snapshot.Location `
 -AllocationMethod Dynamic
```

Retrieve the configuration of the virtual network where the new virtual machine will be hosted. In this example, the new virtual machine is being deployed to the myVnet virtual network:

```
$vnet = Get-AzureRmVirtualNetwork `
 -Name 'myVnet' `
 -ResourceGroupName 'VMLab'
```

Create the NIC in the first (and only) subnet of the myVnet virtual network:

```
$nic = New-AzureRmNetworkInterface `
 -Name 'myNIC4' `
 -ResourceGroupName 'VMLab' `
 -Location $snapshot.Location `
 -SubnetId $vnet.Subnets[0].Id `
 -PublicIpAddressId $pip.Id
```

Add the newly-configured NIC to the configuration for the new myVM4 virtual machine:

```
$vm = Add-AzureRmVMNetworkInterface -VM $vm -Id $nic.Id
```

Whew! That was a lot of work! That said, the configuration for the new virtual machine is now set. Let's create the actual virtual machine.

Creating the virtual machine

With the configuration set for the new virtual machine (myVM4), we can now create the new virtual machine by running the New-AzureRmVm command, referencing the virtual machine configuration stored in the $vm variable:

```
New-AzureRmVM `
 -VM $vm `
 -ResourceGroupName 'VMLab' `
 -Location $snapshot.Location
```

The process takes a few minutes to complete, since we are deploying a new virtual machine. However, when it completes, you'll be notified on the screen:

```
RequestId IsSuccessStatusCode StatusCode ReasonPhrase
--------- ------------------- ---------- ------------
                         True         OK OK
```

Once the deployment process completes, you can confirm the existence and status of the new virtual machine by running the `Get-AzureRmVm` command:

```
Get-AzureRmVm -name MyVM4 -ResourceGroupName VMLab -status
```

This command will retrieve the current status of the new `myVM4` virtual machine.

Your turn

- **Project**: Snapshots
- **Project goal**: Create a virtual machine, snapshot it, create a disk from the snapshot, and deploy a new VM from the disk
- **Key commands**:
    - New-AzureRmResourceGroup
    - Get-AzureRmVm
    - New-AzureRmSnapshotConfig
    - New-AzureRmSnapshot
    - Get-AzureRmSnapshot
    - New-AzureRmDiskConfig
    - New-AzureRmDisk
    - New-AzureRmVMConfig
    - Set-AzureRmVMOSDisk
    - New-AzureRmPublicIpAddress
    - Get-AzureRmVirtualNetwork
    - New-AzureRmNetworkInterface
    - Add-AzureRmVMNetworkInterface
    - New-AzureRmVM
    - Get-AzureRmVm
    - Remove-AzureRmResourceGroup

- **General steps**:
    1. Create a resource group
    2. Deploy a virtual machine with a default configuration
    3. Take a snapshot of the virtual machine
    4. Delete the virtual machine
    5. Deploy a second virtual machine from the snapshot
    6. Delete the resource group and all resources

- **Validation**: Ensure that the new virtual machine deploys successfully by logging into it after deploying it from the snapshot
- **Reference info**: The *Snapshotting an Azure VM Disk* and *Creating VMs from Snapshots* sections

Encrypting virtual machine disks

If you are after enhanced security for your Azure virtual machines, disk encryption should be something you are considering. By leveraging the Azure Key Vault, you can attain enhanced security and compliance by encrypting the disks of your Windows and Linux virtual machines in Azure, using keys that are stored in the vault. Access can also be audited.

Follow the steps in this tutorial to learn how to encrypt virtual disks on an Azure virtual machine, using PowerShell.

An Overview of disk Encryption

While at rest, virtual disks on an Azure virtual machine are encrypted, using Bitlocker. This process incurs no Azure charges. Cryptographic keys, stored in the Azure Key Vault, are used to encrypt and decrypt the virtual disks that are attached to the VM. An Azure Active Directory service principal provides a secure mechanism for issuing these cryptographic keys, as VMs are powered on and off.

Encrypting an Azure VM disk requires the following:

- Deployment of an Azure Key Vault
- Creation of a cryptographic key in the Azure Key Vault
- Configuration of a cryptographic key for use with disk encryption
- An Azure Active Directory service principal with appropriate permissions

With these requirements in place, an Azure virtual machine disk can be encrypted by issuing the `Set-AzureRmVMDiskEncryptionExtension` command to encrypt the disk, specifying the correct Azure Active Directory service principal, and specifying the cryptographic key to be used for the encryption.

Upon commencement of the disk-encryption process, the Azure Active Directory service principal requests the specified key from Azure Key Vault and then the disk is encrypted using the specified key.

Encryption process

Disk encryption relies on two key components: **Azure Key Vault** and **Azure Active Directory**. The Azure Key Vault is used to protect the keys and secrets that are used for disk encryption and decryption. A Key Vault dedicated to disk encryption is not necessary, so if an existing vault exists, it can be used for disk-encryption purposes.

Azure Active Directory handles the exchange of keys and authentication. Because a secure method for requesting and issuing the required encryption keys is necessary, this functionality is provided by the service principle.

Requirements and limitations

Disk encryption in Azure supports encryption on new Windows virtual machines deployed from either Azure Marketplace images or from custom VHD images. Encrypting disks on existing Windows virtual machines in Azure and those configured using Storage Spaces is also supported. However, all resources, including the Key Vault, Storage Account, and the Virtual Machine whose disk is being encrypted must all belong to the same subscription and reside in the same region.

As of this writing, disk encryption is not currently supported in the following scenarios:

- Basic tier virtual machines
- Classic VMs
- Updating the cryptographic keys on an already-encrypted virtual machine
- Integration with on-premises KMS

Essentially, as long as the virtual machine being encrypted is standard-tier on the Resource Manager platform, support is there for disk encryption.

Creating the Azure Key Vault and keys

Before launching the disk-encryption process, ensure that the latest version of the Azure PowerShell module is installed. For more information, see **How to install and configure Azure PowerShell** at `https://www.udemy.com/creating-and-managing-azure-virtual-machines-with-powershell/?couponCode=GENERALOFFER`. Throughout this tutorial, the following naming will be used:

- **Resource Group**: `VMLab`
- **Key Vault Name**: `BlueWidgetKeyVault999`
- **Virtual Machine**: `myVM4`
- **Key Name**: `myKey`
- **App Name**: `myApp`

Because a key vault is required to store the keys that will be used to encrypt the disk, create an Azure Key Vault to store the keys. To do so, enable the Azure Key Vault provider within your Azure subscription by running the following three commands:

```
$rgName = "VMLab"
$location = "East US"
Register-AzureRmResourceProvider `
-ProviderNamespace "Microsoft.KeyVault"
```

The first two commands are used to set variables that will be used during the process. The third command, `Register-AzureRmResourceProvider`, adds key vault support.

After preparing the environment with the preceding commands, create an Azure Key Vault, using the `New-AzureRmKeyVault` command, enabling the key vault for use with disk encryption at the same time. Run the following two commands to deploy the key vault:

```
$keyVaultName = "BlueWidgetKeyVault999"
New-AzureRmKeyVault -Location $location `
-ResourceGroupName $rgName `
-VaultName $keyVaultName `
-EnabledForDiskEncryption
```

Although keys can be stored in the vault using either software or HSM protection, we'll use software protection, since HSM requires a premium key vault—which incurs additional costs.

With the key vault deployed, create an encryption key in the key vault by running the `Add-AzureKeyVaultKey` command:

```
Add-AzureKeyVaultKey -VaultName $keyVaultName `
 -Name "myKey" `
 -Destination "Software"
```

The preceding command creates a new software-protected key, called `myKey`. This is the key that will be used to encrypt the disk later in this tutorial.

Creating the Azure Active Directory service principal

With the encryption key created and stored in the Key Vault, a service principal must be created. The service principal is an account that handles the authentication and exchange of keys during the encryption and decryption processes. This Azure Active Directory service principal allows Azure to request the required keys on behalf of the virtual machine being encrypted.

For this tutorial, the default Azure Active Directory instance for my lab subscription will suffice. You can use either your own dedicated Azure AD if you are following along, or you can use the default Azure AD instance that came with your tenant.

To create a service principal in Azure Active Directory, run the following four commands:

```
$appName = "MyApp"
$securePassword = ConvertTo-SecureString `
-String "RedD1am0nd!" `
-AsPlainText -Force
$app = New-AzureRmADApplication -DisplayName $appName `
-IdentifierUris "http://myApp" `
-Password $securePassword
New-AzureRmADServicePrincipal -ApplicationId $app.ApplicationId
```

The first command stores the name of the app in a variable. The second command creates and stores a password for the service principal in a variable. The third command creates an Azure AD application, called `myApp`, and stores its information in a variable. The last command creates the Azure AD Service principal.

Encrypting and decrypting virtual disks successfully requires permissions on the encryption key stored in Key Vault to allow the Azure Active Directory service principal to read the keys.

Set the permissions on the Key Vault by running the `Set-AzureRmKeyVaultAccessPolicy` command:

```
Set-AzureRmKeyVaultAccessPolicy `
-VaultName $keyvaultName `
-ServicePrincipalName $app.ApplicationId `
-PermissionsToKeys "WrapKey" `
-PermissionsToSecrets "Set"
```

This single-line command sets appropriate permissions on the encryption key so that encryption can be completed successfully.

Encrypting the virtual machine

Encrypting a virtual disk requires all previous components be pulled together. Start by specifying the Azure Active Directory service principal and password, followed by the key vault to store the metadata for the encrypted disks.

Next, specify the cryptographic keys to use for the actual encryption process.

Lastly, specify whether just the OS disk needs to be encrypted, just the data disk, or all disks.

To begin the encryption process for the myVM virtual machine, run the following four commands:

```
$keyVault = Get-AzureRmKeyVault `
-VaultName $keyVaultName `
-ResourceGroupName $rgName
$diskEncryptionKeyVaultUrl = $keyVault.VaultUri
$keyVaultResourceId = $keyVault.ResourceId
$keyEncryptionKeyUrl = (Get-AzureKeyVaultKey `
-VaultName $keyVaultName `
-Name myKey).Key.kid
```

These four commands are used to retrieve the key vault and key that will be used to perform the encryption.

After retrieving the Key Vault and keys, run the `Set-AzureRmVmDiskEncryptionExtension` command to perform the encryption of the myVM4 virtual machine:

```
Set-AzureRmVMDiskEncryptionExtension -ResourceGroupName $rgName `
  -VMName "myVM4" `
  -AadClientID $app.ApplicationId `
```

```
-AadClientSecret `
(New-Object PSCredential `
"user",$securePassword).GetNetworkCredential().Password `
-DiskEncryptionKeyVaultUrl $diskEncryptionKeyVaultUrl `
-DiskEncryptionKeyVaultId $keyVaultResourceId `
-KeyEncryptionKeyUrl $keyEncryptionKeyUrl `
-KeyEncryptionKeyVaultId $keyVaultResourceId
```

This command is, admittedly, a bit long. The process just wouldn't be as fun if it wasn't, right?

The preceding command enables encryption on the myVM virtual machine. The AadClientID switch specifies the client ID of the Azure AD application that has permissions to write to the key vault. The AadClientSecret switch specifies the client secret of the Azure AD application that has permissions to write to the key vault.

The DiskEncryptionKeyVault switches (URL and ID) specify the Key Vault to where the encryption keys should be uploaded, and the KeyEncryptionKey switches (URL and VaultID) specify the key encryption key that is used to wrap and unwrap the virtual machine encryption key:

Accept the prompts and continue with the encryption process. The myVM virtual machine reboots during the process. When the process completes, and the virtual machine has finished rebooting, use the Get-AzureRmVmDiskEncryptionStatus command to check the encryption status of the myVM virtual machine:

```
Get-AzureRmVmDiskEncryptionStatus `
-ResourceGroupName $rgName `
-VMName "myVM4"
```

The preceding command should result in output that shows `OSVolumeEncrypted` and `DataVolumesEncrypted` are encrypted, along with some other information:

```
PS C:\Users\tmitchell> Get-AzureRmVmDiskEncryptionStatus    -ResourceGroupName $rgName -VMName "myVM9"

OsVolumeEncrypted           : Encrypted
DataVolumesEncrypted        : Encrypted
OsVolumeEncryptionSettings  : Microsoft.Azure.Management.Compute.Models.DiskEncryptionSettings
ProgressMessage             : OsVolume: Encrypted, DataVolumes: Encrypted

PS C:\Users\tmitchell>
```

Your turn

- **Project**: Disk Encryption
- **Project goal**: The goal of this project is to successfully deploy an Azure Key Vault and to leverage the key vault to encrypt the VM that you deployed in the **Data Disks** project
- **Key commands:**
    - `Register-AzureRmResourceProvider`
    - `New-AzureRmKeyVault`
    - `Add-AzureKeyVaultKey`
    - `New-AzureRmADApplication`
    - `New-AzureRmADServicePrincipal`
    - `Set-AzureRmKeyVaultAccessPolicy`
    - `Set-AzureRmVMDiskEncryptionExtension`
    - `Get-AzureRmVmDiskEncryptionStatus`
- **General steps:**
    1. Setup an Azure Key Vault
    2. Create an encryption key
    3. Create an Azure AD service principal
    4. Configure encryption
    5. Encrypt the VM that you deployed in the **Data Disks** project
    6. Verify VM is encrypted
    7. Delete the resource group that contains the VM

- **Validation**: Use the `Get-AzureRmVmDiskEncryptionStatus` command to confirm that the OS disk and any data disks attached to the VM are encrypted
- **Reference info**: The *Encrypting Virtual Machine Disks* section

Clearing the Slate

Before working through the exercises in the next section, let's get a level set and clear out all unnecessary resources. You don't want to hit a quota on CPUs or public IPs.

At this point, let's delete the entire VMLab resource group and recreate it. This will delete all resources that currently reside within the resource group.

To delete the VMLab resource group, use the following command:

```
Remove-AzureRmResourceGroup -Name "VMLab" -Force
```

This command will take quite a while to complete, since it is removing several resources from the resource group. Once it completes, run the following command below to create an empty VMLab resource group:

```
New-AzureRmResourceGroup "VMLab" -location "EastUS"
```

After running these commands, you are left with an empty resource group, called VMLab, in the EastUS location.

Summary

In this chapter, we covered several disk-related topics, such as:

- Azure Data Disks
- Snapshotting an Azure VM
- Creating VMs from Snapshots
- Encrypting Virtual Machine Disks

With the skills you learned in this chapter, you can now more easily deploy duplicate VMs and better protect your data via snapshots and encryption.

In the next chapter, we'll cover more advanced, high-availability topics.

High Availability **4**

Welcome to our chapter on **High Availability**, where things are set to get a little more interesting.

When deploying virtual machines in Azure, it's important to consider availability. Whether it's building with unplanned maintenance, outages, or even load balancing in mind, it's critical to build virtual machines that can withstand any scenario.

So, in this chapter, we will cover the following topics:

- Availability sets
- Load balancers

At the end of each section, you will also have the opportunity to work through a hands-on exercise to practice your skills with availability sets and load balancers.

Leveraging availability sets

In this section, you are going to complete some exercises that will teach you how to increase the availability and reliability of your virtual machine solutions on Azure using availability sets.

Availability sets ensure that the virtual machines you deploy in Azure are distributed across multiple isolated hardware nodes in a cluster. Deploying multiple virtual machines in an availability set ensures that if a hardware or software failure within Azure happens, only a subset of the virtual machines are impacted and your overall solution remains available and operational.

In this section, you will learn how to:

- Create an availability set
- Create a VM in an availability set
- Check available VM sizes
- Check Azure Advisor

When you reach the end of these exercises, you should know how to deploy the basic HA functionality that comes with availability sets.

Availability set overview

An availability set is a logical grouping of Azure virtual machines that you can use to ensure that the virtual machines you place within it are isolated from each other when they are deployed within an Azure datacenter. The virtual machines that you place within an availability set are spread across multiple physical servers, racks, storage units, and network switches within Azure. If a failure occurs (whether it's related to Azure or your hardware), only a subset of the virtual machines is impacted. As such, the overall application remains up and running and availability is unaffected. Availability sets are therefore essential to a reliable cloud solution.

When configuring an availability set, a number of fault domains and a number of update domains need to be set. Fault domains define a group of VMs that share a common power source and network switch within the Azure datacenter. Update domains refer to groups of VMs that can be taken down at a single time. Configuring fault and update domains ensures that an application remains running during periods of planned maintenance of the underlying Azure hardware, as well as during unplanned hardware issues.

Use availability sets when you want to deploy reliable virtual machine solutions within Azure.

Creating an availability set

Availability sets are created using the `New-AzureRmAvailabilitySet` command. In this exercise, we are going to provision an availability set and then set the number of update and fault domains as 2. The availability set will be called `myAvailabilitySet`, and it will be deployed to the `VMLab` resource group.

Create a managed availability set

Creating an availability set requires just one command: `New-AzureRmAvailabilitySet`. To create a new availability set called `myAvailabilitySet` in the `VMLab` resource group, run the `New-AzureRmAvailabilitySet` command, as follows:

```
New-AzureRmAvailabilitySet `
-Location "EastUS" `
-Name "myAvailabilitySet" `
-ResourceGroupName "VMLab" `
-Sku aligned `
-PlatformFaultDomainCount 2 `
-PlatformUpdateDomainCount 2
```

This command typically completes rather quickly, and the output on your screen should look something like the following screenshot:

```
PS C:\Users\tmitchell> New-AzureRmAvailabilitySet `
>>    -Location "EastUS" `
>>    -Name "myAvailabilitySet" `
>>    -ResourceGroupName "VMLab" `
>>    -Sku aligned `
>>    -PlatformFaultDomainCount 2 `
>>    -PlatformUpdateDomainCount 2


ResourceGroupName        : VMLab
Id                       : /subscriptions/0aec89a4-d5f8-4343-b43b-1ec899719dfe/resourceGroups/VMLab/providers/Microsoft.Compute/availabilitySets/myA
                           vailabilitySet
Name                     : myAvailabilitySet
Type                     : Microsoft.Compute/availabilitySets
Location                 : eastus
Managed                  : True
Sku                      : Aligned
Tags                     : {}
PlatformFaultDomainCount : 2
PlatformUpdateDomainCount : 2
Statuses                 : []
VirtualMachinesReferences : []
```

If your screen output looks like the preceding screenshot, you've successfully provisioned a new availability set1. You can now deploy virtual machines to your new availability set.

Creating VMs inside an availability set

You can't add an existing virtual machine to an availability set once the virtual machine has been created. Virtual machines must be created within an availability set at the time of deployment to ensure that they are properly distributed across the backend hardware.

The hardware in a location is divided into multiple update domains and fault domains. An **update domain** is a group of VMs and underlying physical hardware that can be rebooted at the same time. Whereas VMs in the same **fault domain** share common storage as well as a common power source and network switch.

When you create a virtual machine with the `New-AzureRmVM` command, the `AvailabilitySetName` switch is used to specify the availability set into which the virtual machine should be deployed.

Deploying a new virtual machine into an availability set is virtually identical to deploying a virtual machine without an availability set. The only difference is the addition of the switch mentioned before.

Before deploying any new virtual machines, you need to set an administrator username and password for the VMs by running the `Get-Credential` command, as follows:

```
$cred = Get-Credential
```

With a local admin credential created, create two new virtual machines in `myAvailabilitySet`. Run the following command twice to create two separate VMs, specifying `myVM1` and `myPublicIP1` for the first virtual machine and `myVM2` and `myPublicIP2` for the second one. All other switch values should remain the same:

```
New-AzureRmVm `
-ResourceGroupName "VMLab" `
-Name "myVM1" `
-Location "EastUS" `
-VirtualNetworkName "myVnet" `
-SubnetName "mySubnet" `
-SecurityGroupName "myNSG" `
-PublicIpAddressName "myPublicIP1" `
-AvailabilitySetName "myAvailabilitySet" `
-Credential $cred `
-AsJob
```

The `-AsJob` parameter creates the virtual machines as background tasks, so control of the PowerShell prompt returns to you. It takes a few minutes to create and configure both virtual machines but, when finished, you have two virtual machines distributed across the underlying hardware.

You can type `Get-AzureRmVm` at the PowerShell prompt to see the status of your VM deployments. The command should look like that in the following screenshot:

ResourceGroupName	Name	Location	VmSize	OsType	NIC	ProvisioningState	Zone
VMLAB	myVM1	eastus	Standard_DS1_v2	Windows	myVM1	Succeeded	
VMLAB	myVM2	eastus	Standard_DS1_v2	Windows	myVM2	Creating	

You can confirm that both machines have been added to the availability set by running the `Get-AzureRmAvailabilitySet` command as follows:

```
Get-AzureRmAvailabilitySet `
-ResourceGroupName "VMLab" `
-Name "MyAvailabilitySet"
```

Running the preceding command should return the following feedback:

```
PS C:\Users\tmitchell> Get-AzureRmAvailabilitySet -ResourceGroupName "VMlab" -Name "MyAvailabilitySet"

ResourceGroupName       : VMLab
Id                      : /subscriptions/0aec89a4-d5f8-4343-b43b-1ec899719dfe/resourceGroups/VMlab/providers/Microsoft.Compute/availabilitySets/myA
                          vailabilitySet
Name                    : myAvailabilitySet
Type                    : Microsoft.Compute/availabilitySets
Location                : eastus
Managed                 : True
Sku                     : Aligned
Tags                    : {}
PlatformFaultDomainCount : 2
PlatformUpdateDomainCount : 2
Statuses                : []
VirtualMachinesReferences : [
                            {
                                "id": "/subscriptions/0aec89a4-d5f8-4343-b43b-1ec899719dfe/resourceGroups/VMLAB/providers/Microsoft.Compute/virtualMa
                            chines/MYVM1"
                            },
                            {
                                "id": "/subscriptions/0aec89a4-d5f8-4343-b43b-1ec899719dfe/resourceGroups/VMLAB/providers/Microsoft.Compute/virtualMa
                            chines/MYVM2"
                            }
                          ]
```

If you've done everything correctly, you should see a screen like the previous screenshot. It should have both `myVM1` and `myVM2` listed in the availability set.

Congratulations! You have now learned how to create an availability set and how to create virtual machines within one.

Your turn

- **Project**: Availability sets
- **Project goal**: The goal of this project is to successfully provision an availability set and to deploy two virtual machines to it
- **Key commands**:
    - New-AzureRmResourceGroup
    - New-AzureRmAvailabilitySet
    - Get-Credential
    - New-AzureRmVm
    - Get-AzureRmAvailabilitySet

- **General steps**:
    1. Create a resource group
    2. Deploy an availability set
    3. Deploy two virtual machines with the default Windows image into the availability set
    4. Install IIS on both virtual machines
- **Validation**: Verify that both virtual machines are listed in the configuration for the availability set
- **Reference info**: Leveraging availability sets

Load balancing Azure VMs

Load balancing provides a higher level of availability by spreading inbound requests across multiple virtual machines. In this section, you will learn about the different components of the Azure load balancer. You will learn how to:

- Create an Azure load balancer
- Create a load balancer health probe
- Create load balancer traffic rules
- Use the Custom Script Extension to create a basic IIS site
- Create virtual machines and attach them to a load balancer
- View a load balancer in action
- Add and remove VMs from a load balancer

There is quite a bit to cover in this section, so it may be a good idea to take a break before getting started.

Azure load balancer overview

An Azure load balancer operates at Layer-4 and provides high availability by distributing incoming traffic among healthy virtual machines. A load balancer health probe monitors a given port on each virtual machine and only distributes traffic to an operational virtual machine.

A typical load balancer configuration can be illustrated like the following diagram:

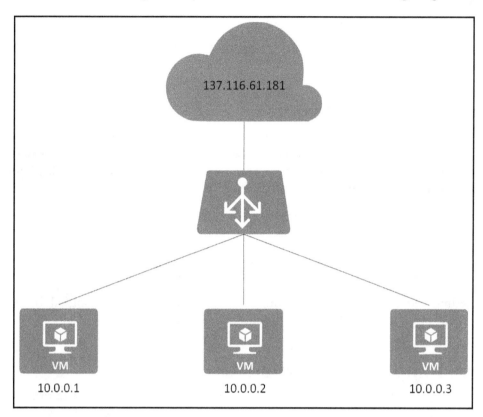

Although the preceding diagram looks pretty simple, there is actually quite a bit going on behind the scenes; a fair of configuration is necessary to make things work.

The deployment of a load balancer requires you to define a frontend IP configuration that contains one or more public IP addresses, which then allows the load balancer (as well as any applications and VMs being load balanced) to be accessed over the internet.

Since virtual machines are connected to a load balancer using their virtual network interface cards, a backend address pool must be created that contains the IP addresses of the virtual NICs connected to the load balancer.

Traffic flow to the load-balanced virtual machines is controlled with defined load balancer rules for specific ports and protocols.

As we've already mentioned, there is quite a bit going on under the hood when it comes to load balancers in Azure.

Creating an Azure load balancer

This section details how you can provision and configure each component of a load balancer. The following exercises create a load balancer called `MyLoadBalancer` in the `VMLab` resource group in the `EastUS` location.

Creating a public IP address

To enable access to an application from the internet via a load balancer, you need to configure a public IP address first. You can create a public IP address with the `New-AzureRmPublicIpAddress` command. The following exercise creates a public IP address named `LBPublicIP` in the `VMLab` resource group:

```
$publicIP = New-AzureRmPublicIpAddress `
 -ResourceGroupName "VMLab" `
 -Location "EastUS" `
 -AllocationMethod "Static" `
 -Name "LBPublicIP"
```

The preceding command essentially creates a static public IP resource that will be assigned to the frontend (in other words, the public side) of the load balancer.

Provisioning the load balancer

With the public IP address provisioned for the load balancer, it's now time to provision the actual load balancer resource. Begin by configuring both the frontend and backend.

Frontend IP configuration

Frontend IP configuration is used to attach the newly-created public IP address (`LBPublicIP`) to the load balancer. This configuration makes the load balancer available publicly. To create a frontend IP configuration, you should use the `New-AzureRmLoadBalancerFrontendIpConfig` command.

Run the following command to create a frontend IP config named `myFrontEnd` and to attach the `LBPublicIP` address to the load balancer:

```
$frontendIP = New-AzureRmLoadBalancerFrontendIpConfig `
 -Name "myFrontEnd" `
 -PublicIpAddress $publicIP
```

The preceding command creates the configuration for the interface that will be used to access the load balancer publicly.

Creating a backend address pool

An Azure load balancer's backend address pool consists of IP addresses associated with the virtual machine NICs. This pool is used to distribute traffic to the virtual machines behind the load balancer. The `New-AzureRmLoadBalancerBackendAddressPoolConfig` command is used to create this pool. The VMs are then attached to this backend pool.

Run the following command to create a backend pool called `myBackEndPool` for the load balancer:

```
$backendPool = New-AzureRmLoadBalancerBackendAddressPoolConfig `
-Name "myBackEndPool"
```

The preceding command doesn't generate any feedback. It just creates a backend configuration and then stores it in the `$backendpool` variable.

Creating the load balancer resource

With the frontend and backend configuration complete, you can now create the load balancer using the `New-AzureRmLoadBalancer` command. Create a load balancer named `myLoadBalancer` that uses the frontend and backend IP pools created in the preceding steps by running the following command:

```
$lb = New-AzureRmLoadBalancer `
-ResourceGroupName "VMLab" `
-Name "myLoadBalancer" `
-Location "EastUS" `
-FrontendIpConfiguration $frontendIP `
-BackendAddressPool $backendPool
```

The preceding command creates a new load balancer resource (`myLoadBalancer`) and stores the configuration in a variable called `$lb`. The configuration of the load balancer includes the frontend and backend settings that were previously configured.

Creating a health probe

To allow the new load balancer to monitor the status of an application or server, we first need to create a health probe. A health probe dynamically adds or removes virtual machines from a load balancer's rotation based on their response to health checks.

By default, a virtual machine is removed from load balancer distribution after two consecutive failures at 15-second intervals. A health probe is typically based on a protocol or a specific health check page for your application in the case of load balancing IIS or web resources.

In the following exercise, we will create a TCP probe that checks for port 80 availability on the virtual machines in the backend pool of the load balancer.

The `Add-AzureRmLoadBalancerProbeConfig` command is used to create a TCP health probe. Create a port-80 TCP health probe for `myLoadBalancer` by running the following command:

```
Add-AzureRmLoadBalancerProbeConfig `
-Name "myHealthProbe" `
-LoadBalancer $lb `
-Protocol tcp `
-Port 80 `
-IntervalInSeconds 15 `
-ProbeCount 2
```

After creating the health probe, run the following command to apply the probe to the load balancer and to update it:

```
Set-AzureRmLoadBalancer -LoadBalancer $lb
```

Running the preceding command should provide feedback like that in the following screenshot:

```
PS C:\Users\tmitchell> Set-AzureRmLoadBalancer -LoadBalancer $lb

Name                      : myLoadBalancer
ResourceGroupName         : VMLab
Location                  : eastus
Id                        : /subscriptions/0aec89a4-d5f8-4343-b43b-1ec899719dfe/resourceGroups/VMLab/providers/Microsoft.Network/loadBalancers/myLoad
                            alancer
Etag                      : W/"b6dace60-6a59-4e51-aeb4-cc9d20a31d6c"
ResourceGuid              : 2844fcae-cf15-4b51-96d2-560fc2d5cccb
ProvisioningState         : Succeeded
Tags                      :
FrontendIpConfigurations  : [
                              {
                                "Zones": [],
                                "Name": "myFrontEndPool",
                                "Etag": "W/\"b6dace60-6a59-4e51-aeb4-cc9d20a31d6c\"",
                                "Id": "/subscriptions/0aec89a4-d5f8-4343-b43b-1ec899719dfe/resourceGroups/VMLab/providers/Microsoft.Network/loadBalar
                            ers/myLoadBalancer/frontendIPConfigurations/myFrontEndPool",
                                "PrivateIpAllocationMethod": "Dynamic",
                                "PublicIpAddress": {
```

After setting the load balancer's configuration, you should receive feedback that it was successful.

Creating a load balancer rule

With the load balancer provisioned, load balancer rules now need to be configured. Rules are used to define how traffic is distributed to the virtual machines sitting behind the load balancer. Defining rules is a two-part process; you need to define the frontend IP configuration for the inbound traffic and the configuration for the backend IP pool in order to receive the traffic. Source and destination ports must also be configured. Ensuring that only healthy virtual machines receive traffic through the load balancer requires you to also define which health probe to use.

The `Add-AzureRmLoadBalancerRuleConfig` command is used to create a load balancer rule. Run the following command to create a load balancer rule named `myLoadBalancerRule` that balances traffic on TCP port 80. The command will store the rule settings in the `$probe` variable, which is used in the following command:

```
$probe = Get-AzureRmLoadBalancerProbeConfig `
-LoadBalancer $lb `
-Name "myHealthProbe"
```

Run the following command to assign the newly-created rule to the load balancer:

```
Add-AzureRmLoadBalancerRuleConfig `
-Name "myLoadBalancerRule" `
-LoadBalancer $lb `
-FrontendIpConfiguration $lb.FrontendIpConfigurations[0] `
-BackendAddressPool $lb.BackendAddressPools[0] `
-Protocol Tcp `
-FrontendPort 80 `
-BackendPort 80 `
-Probe $probe
```

The preceding command adds the new rule to the load balancer using the `Add-AzureRmLoadBalancerRuleConfig` command. If you've completed the exercise correctly, you should see feedback like that in the following screenshot:

```
                              "BackendPort": 80,
                              "Protocol": "Tcp"
                           }
                        ]
                        ]
    Probes                : [
                           {
                              "Name": "myHealthProbe",
                              "Id": "/subscriptions/0aec89a4-d5f8-4343-b43b-1ec899719dfe/resourceGroups/VMLab/providers/Microsoft.Network/loadBalanc
    ers/myLoadBalancer/probes/myHealthProbe",
                              "Protocol": "tcp",
                              "Port": 80,
                              "IntervalInSeconds": 15,
                              "NumberOfProbes": 2
```

At this point, the load balancer has been created and the configuration updated, so it's now time to update the actual load balancer with the updated configuration.

Updating the load balancer

With all of the load balancer configurations complete, the load balancer itself can now be updated with the configuration set. This is completed by running the `Set-AzureRmLoadBalancer` command.

Run the following command to update the `MyLoadBalancer` load balancer:

```
Set-AzureRmLoadBalancer -LoadBalancer $lb
```

Running the preceding command completes the configuration and deployment of the load balancer. At this point, it's time to deploy the virtual machines and connect them to the load balancer.

Network resources

Before you deploy and attach virtual machines to your new load balancer, the supporting network resources need to be prepared.

Preparing network resources

Because we already have a virtual network in place, we don't need to create one. Instead, we will deploy our new load-balanced virtual machines to `mySubnet` on the `myVnet` virtual network. To do this, we need to first store the virtual network and virtual subnet configurations in variables, so they can be referenced later.

Getting network configuration

To retrieve the configuration of the `myVnet` virtual network, you will need to use the `Get-AzureRmVirtualNetwork` command. This will retrieve the configuration of the `MyVnet` virtual network and store it in a variable called `$vnet`.

Run the following command to retrieve the `myVnet` configuration:

```
$vnet = Get-AzureRmVirtualNetwork `
-ResourceGroupName "VMLab" `
-Name "myVnet"
```

The preceding command will not produce any output onscreen as it is only pulling configuration information into a variable.

Getting subnet configuration

In addition to the virtual network configuration, the subnet configuration must also be retrieved and stored in a variable for later modification. The `Get-AzureRmVirtualNetworkSubnetConfig` command is used to retrieve the subnet configuration.

Run the following command to retrieve the configuration of `mySubnet`:

```
$subnetConfig = Get-AzureRmVirtualNetworkSubnetConfig `
-Name "mySubnet" -VirtualNetwork $vnet
```

The preceding command retrieves the configuration information for `mySubnet` and stores it in the `$subnetconfig` variable.

Creating virtual NICs

Virtual NICs are created with `New-AzureRmNetworkInterface`. Run the following command twice—once for each virtual machine that will attach to the load balancer. The names to use for the NICs should be `myVM3` and `myVM4`, so that they match the new VMs being deployed:

```
New-AzureRmNetworkInterface `
-ResourceGroupName "VMLab" `
-Name myVM3 `
-Location "EastUS" `
-Subnet $vnet.Subnets[0] `
-LoadBalancerBackendAddressPool $lb.BackendAddressPools[0]
```

It's important that you call your virtual NICs myVM3 and myVM4, because when you deploy the virtual machines in the following step, the process will automatically attach the NICs to the corresponding VMs. Instead of creating new NICs, the virtual machine deployment process will simply update the existing NICs that you've provisioned. This simplifies the process of creating and attaching NICs.

Creating virtual machines

With the load balancer in place and configured, it's now time to deploy the virtual machines that the load balancer will load balance. The exercises in these upcoming sections will walk you through the process of creating an availability set (per best practice) as well as the deployment of the load-balanced virtual machines.

Creating an availability set

You learned about availability sets earlier in this book. To conform to best practice, create a new availability set for your load-balanced virtual machines by running the New-AzureRmAvailabilitySet command.

Run the following command to create an availability set named newAvailabilitySet:

```
$availabilitySet = New-AzureRmAvailabilitySet `
-ResourceGroupName "VMLab" `
-Name "newAvailabilitySet" `
-Location "EastUS" `
-Sku aligned `
-PlatformFaultDomainCount 2 `
-PlatformUpdateDomainCount 2
```

The resulting availability set will host the load-balanced virtual machines that we are about to deploy.

Deploying virtual machines

Now it's time to set an administrator username and password for the VMs with Get-Credential, as follows:

```
$cred = Get-Credential
```

Create two VMs using the following command, repeating it for each new virtual machine. Call the first virtual machine myVM3 and the second virtual machine myVM4:

```
 New-AzureRmVm `
-ResourceGroupName "VMLab" `
-Name "myVM3" `
-Location "EastUS" `
-VirtualNetworkName "myVnet" `
-SubnetName "mySubnet" `
-SecurityGroupName "newNSG" `
-OpenPorts 80 `
-AvailabilitySetName "newAvailabilitySet" `
-Credential $cred `
-AsJob
```

The -AsJob parameter creates the virtual machine as a background task, so the PowerShell prompts return to you. You can view the details of background jobs with the Job cmdlet. Note that it takes a few minutes to create and configure VMs.

Run the Get-AzureRmVm -status command to ensure both new VMs are deployed and running before continuing.

It's important that you call your new virtual machines myVM3 and myVM4. If the names of your new VMs do not match the names of the NICs you deployed, the virtual machine deployment process will create new NICs instead of updating the existing NICs—more importantly, your virtual machines will not be attached to the load balancer.

Installing IIS on the VMs

To test the load balancer, you need to be able to determine which virtual machine you are connecting to while testing. To do this, you need to install IIS on each virtual machine. Although this can be done via Custom Script Extensions, we haven't yet covered Custom Script Extensions. As such, for this exercise, just install IIS manually on each virtual machine (MyVM3 and MyVM4) using Server Manager.

Installing and configuring IIS

To install and configure IIS on the two load-balanced virtual machines, RDP into MyVM2 and use that as a jump box to RDP into the private IP address of MyVM3. You can get the private IP address for MyVM3 by running the following command:

```
(Get-AzureRmNetworkInterface `
-Name myvm3 `
-ResourceGroupName vmlab).IpConfigurations.PrivateIpAddress
```

After RDPing into MyVM3, install IIS on the server. When the installation of IIS is complete, open Notepad on the MyVM3 virtual machine and create a file called Default.htm in the C:\inetpub\wwwroot folder. Edit Default.htm so that the only text in the file is MYVM3.

Repeat this process for MyVM4, ensuring that the Default.htm file for MyVM4 consists only of MYVM4.

Can you guess why you need to use MyVM2 as a jump box, and why you have to RDP to the private IPs of MyVM3 and MyVM4 rather than their public IPs?

It's because MyVM3 and MyVM4 both sit behind the load balancer, and we have not opened RDP via the Network Security Group. Additionally, since both are behind the load balancer, their public IPs are the same.

Once IIS has been installed on both VMs, and the Default.htm file has been created on each machine, you can test the load balancer.

Completing these steps modifies the default page on each VM to display each respective virtual machine's name. This will allow you to easily see which virtual machine you are connecting to when you move on to test the load balancer.

Testing the load balancer

Now that the load balancer is configured, and you have two virtual machines being load balanced by it, it's time to test the load balancer's functionality. Retrieve the public IP address of your load balancer with the following command, Get-AzureRmPublicIPAddress:

```
Get-AzureRmPublicIPAddress `
-ResourceGroupName "VMLab" `
-Name "LBPublicIP" | select IpAddress
```

After retrieving the load balancer's public IP address, you can access that public IP address in a web browser. When the default web page is displayed, the hostname of the virtual machine you are connecting to through the load balancer will be displayed.

You might have to refresh your browser numerous times, or even stop one virtual machine, to see it connect to the second virtual machine.

Adding and removing VMs

There may be occasions where you need to perform maintenance on the virtual machines that are running your load-balanced application. Be it OS patching, software upgrades, or otherwise, you will find yourself needing to perform maintenance.

After performing said maintenance, you'll need to be able to re-attach the virtual machine to the load balancer.

In the next few exercises, you will learn how to remove a virtual machine from a load balancer and how to *add* a virtual machine to a load balancer.

Removing a VM from the load balancer

Removing a virtual machine from a load balancer requires you to retrieve the configuration of the attached NIC, detach the NIC from the load balancer backend address pool, and then to update the NIC. This process requires three commands.

To retrieve the network interface card configuration, run the `Get-AzureRmNetworkInterface` command as follows:

```
$nic = Get-AzureRmNetworkInterface `
-ResourceGroupName "VMLab" `
-Name "myVM4"
```

The preceding command retrieves the configuration of the NIC for the `myVM4` virtual machine and stores it in a variable called `$nic`.

After retrieving the NIC configuration, alter it so that it's no longer connected to the backend pool by setting the `LoadBalancerBackendAddressPools` property of the virtual NIC to `$null`, as follows:

```
$nic.Ipconfigurations[0].LoadBalancerBackendAddressPools=$null
```

Finally, update the virtual NIC with the following `Set-AzureRmNetworkInterface` command:

```
Set-AzureRmNetworkInterface -NetworkInterface $nic
```

Performing these steps will disconnect the myVM4 virtual machine from the load balancer. To confirm, close your browser, re-open it, and browse your load balancer's IP address. The only virtual machine that should be servicing your requests is `myVM3`.

Adding a VM to the load balancer

Whether it's because of virtual machine maintenance or the need to expand your capacity, you will need to know how to add a virtual machine to the load balancer. To do so, simply set the `LoadBalancerBackendAddressPools` property of the virtual NIC to the `BackendAddressPool`.

Re-attaching `myVM4` to the load balancer requires four commands.

Begin the process of re-attaching myVM4 by running the following command:

```
$lb = Get-AzureRMLoadBalancer `
-ResourceGroupName VMLab `
-Name myLoadBalancer
```

The preceding command retrieves the load balancer configuration for `myLoadBalancer` and stores it in the `$lb` variable.

After retrieving the load balancer configuration, run the following command to retrieve the configuration of the virtual NIC for `myVM4`, and then store it in a variable called `$nic`:

```
$nic = Get-AzureRmNetworkInterface `
-ResourceGroupName "VMLab" `
-Name "myVM4"
```

After retrieving the NIC configuration with the preceding command, run the following command to attach the NIC to the backend pool of the load balancer:

```
$nic.IpConfigurations[0].LoadBalancerBackendAddressPools `
=$lb.BackendAddressPools[0]
```

After connecting the NIC for `myVM4` to the backend pool of the load balancer with the previous command, run the following code to update the NIC configuration to complete the process:

```
Set-AzureRmNetworkInterface -NetworkInterface $nic
```

After completing the preceding step, you can restart your browser to confirm that both virtual machines can now service requests. You can also run `Get-AzureRmLoadBalancer -Status` for connection confirmation.

In this section, which was admittedly quite arduous, you created a load balancer, attached virtual machines to it, and then removed virtual machines from it.

You also learned how to:

- Create an Azure load balancer
- Create a load balancer health probe
- Create load balancer traffic rules
- Create virtual machines and attach them to a load balancer
- View a load balancer in action
- Add and remove VMs from a load balancer

This section was quite long, so it may be best reviewing it more than once.

Your turn

- **Project**: Load balancing VMs.
- **Project goal**: The goal of this project is to successfully deploy a load balancer and to attach two existing virtual machines (that are running IIS) to it.
- **Key commands**:
  - `New-AzureRmPublicIpAddress`
  - `New-AzureRmLoadBalancerFrontendIpConfig`
  - `New-AzureRmLoadBalancerBackendAddressPoolConfig`
  - `New-AzureRmLoadBalancer`
  - `Add-AzureRmLoadBalancerProbeConfig`
  - `Set-AzureRmLoadBalancer`
  - `Get-AzureRmLoadBalancerProbeConfig`
  - `Add-AzureRmLoadBalancerRuleConfig`
  - `Set-AzureRmLoadBalancer`
  - `Get-AzureRmVirtualNetwork`
  - `Get-AzureRmVirtualNetworkSubnetConfig`
  - `New-AzureRmNetworkInterface`
  - `New-AzureRmAvailabilitySet`
  - `Get-Credential`
  - `New-AzureRmVm`
  - `Remove-AzureRmResourceGroup`

- **General steps**:
    1. Deploy a load balancer to the resource group deployed in the **availability sets** project
    2. Attach both virtual machines from the **availability sets** project to the load balancer
    3. Verify load balancer functionality
    4. Delete the resource group and all resources
- **Validation**: Verify that the load balancer sends traffic to both virtual machines by accessing the public IP of the load balancer. Note which virtual machine responds and then stop it. Close your browser and visit the public IP of the load balancer once more to confirm that the second virtual machine responds.
- **Reference info**: Load balancing Azure VMs.

Summary

Congratulations on completing this chapter! In this chapter, we covered availability sets and load balancers. Learning how to leverage these resources enables you to ensure a more robust Azure environment that can withstand both expected and unexpected outages.

In the next chapter, we'll cover a bunch of other cool stuff, so head on over to Chapter 5, *Other Cool Stuff*, now!

5
Other Cool Stuff

Now it's time for some **other cool stuff!**

In this chapter, we're going to cover several features and capabilities that are slightly beyond the scope of previous chapters; we'll walk through the following topics:

- Adding and removing NICs
- VM tagging
- Redeploying VMs
- Custom Script Extensions
- Resetting the admin password

In this chapter, you'll also have the opportunity to perform some of these tasks thanks to a number of hands-on exercises. After finishing this chapter, you will have learned several skills that will prove useful on a day-to-day basis.

Adding an NIC to a virtual machine

Adding a virtual NIC to an existing virtual machine can be a bit complex when using PowerShell, so in this section, we'll cover the process of creating a new virtual NIC and how to connect it to an existing virtual machine.

To add a new virtual NIC to an existing **virtual machine (VM)**, the VM must first be deallocated. After the VM has been deallocated, the NIC is added to the VM, which can then be started up once more. Different VM sizes support varying numbers of NICs, so as such, the VM we'll work with in the following exercises will be sized to support multiple NICs.

Preparing the virtual machine

To begin the process of adding a new virtual NIC to the myVM1 virtual machine, run the Stop-AzureRmVm command to stop and deallocate the virtual machine:

```
Stop-AzureRmVM -Name "myVM1" -ResourceGroupName "VMLab"
```

After ensuring that myVM1 has been stopped and deallocated, retrieve the existing configuration of the virtual machine by running the Get-AzureRmVm command:

```
$vm = Get-AzureRmVm -Name "myVM1" -ResourceGroupName "VMLab"
```

The preceding command stores the VM's information in a variable called $vm.

Retrieving Vnet and subnet information

With the virtual machine retrieved and stored in the $vm variable, it's now time to run two commands that will retrieve information relating to the virtual network and subnet. As you can see in the following commands, we are going to attach the new NIC to the mySubnet subnet on the myVnet virtual network:

```
$myVnet = Get-AzureRmVirtualNetwork `
 -Name "myVnet" `
 -ResourceGroupName "VMLab"
$subnet = $myVnet.Subnets|?{$_.Name -eq 'mySubnet'}
```

The preceding commands store the virtual network and subnet information in variables so that they can be modified when the NIC is attached.

Creating a virtual NIC and attaching it to the subnet

Run the following command to create a new NIC called myNewNIC. The command also attaches the NIC to the virtual network, as follows:

```
$newNic = New-AzureRmNetworkInterface -ResourceGroupName "VMLab" `
 -Name "myNewNIC" `
 -Location "EastUs" `
 -SubnetId $subnet.Id
```

After creating the NIC and attaching it to the virtual network, the NIC can be added to the myVM1 virtual machine.

Adding NICs to VMs

To add a new NIC to the `myVM1` virtual machine, run the following four commands:

```
$nicId = (Get-AzureRmNetworkInterface `
 -ResourceGroupName "VMLab" `
 -Name "MyNewNIC").Id

$VM = Add-AzureRmVMNetworkInterface -VM $VM -Id $nicId

$VM.NetworkProfile.NetworkInterfaces.Item(0).primary = $true

Update-AzureRmVM -ResourceGroupName "vmlab" -VM $VM
```

The first command retrieves the Azure ID of the newly created NIC. The NIC is then added to the `myVM1` virtual machine configuration with the second command. With the third command, the existing NIC (the one originally created with the VM) is set as the primary NIC (note that all VMs must have a primary NIC). Finally, the fourth command, `Update-AzureRmVm`, is used to update the `myVM1` virtual machine configuration to include the newly attached NIC.

A quick check of the network settings for `MyVM3` in the Azure portal should show the new NIC attached, as follows:

Tagging with PowerShell

Tags in Azure provide admins with a way of organizing Azure resources logically, using user-defined properties. Tags can be applied to entire resource groups or to resources directly. Using tags allows you to select resources or resource groups from the console, web portal, PowerShell, and even through the API. Tags are commonly used to organize resources for billing and management.

Each tag consists of a name and a value. For example, many admins will tag their `production` resources in Azure with an `Environment` tag and a value of `Production`. Doing so allows you to identify easily and group production resources.

By using tags, you can retrieve all related resources in an Azure subscription, based on the values of the tags. Tags can be placed on Compute, Network, and Storage resources during creation, as well as after resource creation, using PowerShell. This section will concentrate on how to view and edit tags placed on virtual machines.

How to tag a VM with PowerShell

Tagging a virtual machine requires you to retrieve the virtual machine, load all existing tags into a variable, update the list with any new tags, and then assign the newly updated list of tags to the virtual machine. This process is required because when you add a tag to a resource, the new addition overwrites any tags currently assigned to the resource. By extracting the existing tags, updating them, and then reassigning them, you can be sure that no tags are lost.

To assign a new tag to a virtual machine, retrieve the virtual machine with the `Get-AzureRmVm` cmdlet, as follows:

```
Get-AzureRmVM -ResourceGroupName "VMLab" -Name "MyVM3"
```

If your virtual machine already contains tags, you will see existing tags assigned to your virtual machine. If it has not been tagged, the `tags` field will be empty, as seen in the following screenshot:

```
ResourceGroupName        : VMLab
Id                       : /subscriptions/0aec89a4-d5f8-4343-b43b-1ec899719dfe/resourceGroups/VMLab/providers/Microsoft.Compute
VmId                     : 8e3c6f95-d646-4850-9250-7995446f024c
Name                     : myVM3
Type                     : Microsoft.Compute/virtualMachines
Location                 : eastus
Tags                     : {}
AvailabilitySetReference : {Id}
Extensions               : {IIS}
HardwareProfile          : {VmSize}
NetworkProfile           : {NetworkInterfaces}
OSProfile                : {ComputerName, AdminUsername, WindowsConfiguration, Secrets}
ProvisioningState        : Succeeded
StorageProfile           : {ImageReference, OsDisk, DataDisks}
```

As you can see, you use the `Set-AzureRmResource` command to add tags via PowerShell. Adding additional tags to a virtual machine using PowerShell is illustrated in the following snippet.

The first step to tagging a virtual machine is to store all existing tags assigned to it in a variable. Run the following command to store all existing tags for the MyVM3 virtual machine in a variable called `$tags`:

```
$tags = (Get-AzureRmResource `
  -ResourceGroupName VMLab `
  -ResourceType Microsoft.Compute/virtualMachines `
  -Name MyVM3).Tags
```

Running the following command outputs whatever tags are stored:

```
$tags
```

In our case, there are no tags yet, as shown in the following screenshot:

```
PS C:\Users\tmitchell> $tags = (Get-AzureRmResource -ResourceGroupName VMLab -Name MyVM3).Tags
PS C:\Users\tmitchell> $tags
PS C:\Users\tmitchell>
```

After pulling all of the existing tags into our $tags variable, we need to add our additional tag to the $tags variable using the following command:

```
$tags += @{Name="Location";Value="MyLocation"}
```

As you can see, this command adds a tag called Location to the list of tags for MyVM3 that is stored in our variable. It also sets the value of this tag to MyLocation.

The following command assigns the updated list of tags to the MyVM3 virtual machine:

```
Set-AzureRmResource `
 -ResourceGroupName VMLab `
 -Name MyVM3 `
 -ResourceType "Microsoft.Compute/VirtualMachines" `
 -Tag $tags
```

After updating the tags on MyVM3 with the preceding command, you can run the Get-AzureRmResource command to confirm that the new Location tag has been successfully added, as follows:

```
(Get-AzureRmResource `
 -ResourceGroupName VMLab `
 -ResourceType "Microsoft.Compute/VirtualMachines" `
 -Name MyVM3).Tags
```

You may sometimes find yourself in a position where you need to delete tags from virtual machines; the Set-AzureRmResource command will do this, as follows:

```
Set-AzureRmResource `
 -ResourceGroupName VMLab `
 -Name MyVM3 `
 -ResourceType "Microsoft.Compute/VirtualMachines" `
 -Tag @{}
```

So, running the `Set-AzureRmResource` command should result in output similar to that
which is shown in the following screenshot:

```
PS C:\Users\tmitchell> Set-AzureRmResource `
>> -ResourceGroupName VMLab `
>> -Name MyVM3 `
>> -ResourceType "Microsoft.Compute/VirtualMachines" `
>> -Tag @{}

Confirm
Are you sure you want to update the following resource: /subscriptions/0aec89a4-d5f8-4343-b43b-1ec899719dfe/resourceGroups/VMLab/providers/Microsoft.Compute/VirtualMachines/MyVM3
[Y] Yes  [N] No  [S] Suspend  [?] Help (default is "Y"): y
```

Confirm that all tags are gone for MyVM3 by running the following command:

```
(Get-AzureRmResource `
 -ResourceGroupName VMLab `
 -ResourceType "Microsoft.Compute/VirtualMachines" `
 -Name MyVM3).Tags
```

Redeploying a virtual machine

There will be times when you have issues trying to connect to an Azure virtual machine via
RDP. Finding access to applications running on a virtual machine can also be problematic.
If you encounter these types of issues, redeploying the virtual machine may help.

Redeploying a virtual machine simply moves the virtual machine to a new node within
Azure and then powers it back on. Its configuration settings and associated resources are all
retained. You could liken this process to using the vMotion feature in VMware when
migrating a virtual machine to a different host.

One thing to keep in mind, however, is that when a virtual machine is redeployed, the
temporary disk is lost, and any dynamic IP addresses associated with the virtual network
interfaces are updated (and could therefore change). This is no different to when a virtual
machine is topped and deallocated.

Run the following command to redeploy the myVM4 virtual machine:

```
Set-AzureRmVM -Redeploy -ResourceGroupName "VMLab" -Name "myVM4"
```

As shown in the preceding code, the `Set-AzureRmVm` command shuts the myVM4 virtual
machine down, moves it to another node in Azure, and then turns it back on.

Now it's your turn!

- **Project**: Redeploying VMs
- **Project goal**: The goal of this project is to redeploy a virtual machine successfully
- **Key commands**:
    - `New-AzureRmResourceGroup`
    - `New-AzureRmVm`
    - `Set-AzureRmVm`
    - `Remove-AzureRmResourceGroup`
- **General steps**:
    1. Create a resource group
    2. Deploy a virtual machine with a default configuration
    3. Redeploy the virtual machine
    4. Delete the resource group and all resources
- **Validation**: Verify that you can RDP into the virtual machine after redeploying it
- **Reference information**: The *Redeploying a virtual machine* section

Custom Script Extensions

In a production environment, it will sometimes be necessary to deploy a server role to several virtual machines quickly. You might also need to install an application to multiple servers with an identical configuration. An elegant remote installation solution in cases such as these is the use of Custom Script Extensions for Windows.

Leveraging Custom Script Extensions allows you to, among other things, remotely install server roles, features, and applications right from your PowerShell session.

In this section, you will learn how to enable the File Services role on a virtual machine using a Custom Script Extension.

Custom Script Extensions – an overview

A Custom Script Extension is a piece of software that runs configuration tasks or downloads preconfigured scripts to a virtual machine and then runs those scripts. Custom Script Extensions are typically used to automate the configuration of server settings after a virtual machine has been deployed. Extensions can also be used to install software automatically and to handle various management tasks.

Scripts used by the extension can be downloaded from Azure Storage, GitHub, or can even be provided to the Azure portal when the extension is running. This section will cover the use of Custom Script Extensions when configuring a virtual machine in Azure.

The Custom Script Extension itself works with both Windows and Linux virtual machines and can be run via PowerShell, the Azure CLI, and even the Azure Portal. It can also be called from the Azure Virtual Machine REST API. We'll be covering the use of Custom Script Extensions in a Windows environment, using PowerShell, in this tutorial.

Enabling print services with CSE

To enable print services, we need to tell the Custom Script Extension what to run. In this exercise, we need to tell CSE to launch PowerShell, and once launched, call the Add-WindowsFeature command, which in turn specifies Print-Services. By running the following command, we store the full PowerShell command in a variable called CSESettings:

```
$CSESettings = '{"commandToExecute":"powershell Add-WindowsFeature Print-Services"}'
```

With the Add-WindowsFeature PowerShell command stored, the following Set-AzureRmVmExtension command can be used to enable the Custom Script Extension on the MyVM1 virtual machine:

```
Set-AzureRmVMExtension `
 -ExtensionName "PrintServer" `
 -ResourceGroupName VMLab `
 -VMName MyVM1 `
 -Publisher "Microsoft.Compute" `
 -ExtensionType "CustomScriptExtension" `
 -TypeHandlerVersion 1.4 `
 -SettingString $CSESettings `
 -Location "East US"
```

In the preceding command, the -ExtensionName switch is used to specify a name for the extension being deployed. The -Publisher switch specifies the name of the extension publisher, and the -ExtensionType switch specifies the type of extension being deployed. The -TypeHandlerVersion switch specifies the version of the extension to use, and the -SettingString switch specifies the configuration for the extension. In this case, it references our CSESettings variable, as shown in the following screenshot:

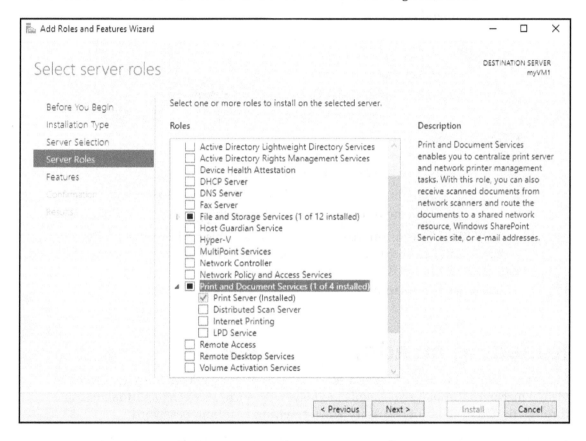

If you followed the instructions in this exercise correctly, you should see the print server listed as **Installed** in the **Roles** and **Features** Wizard on MyVM1.

Now it's your turn!

- **Project**: Custom Script Extensions
- **Project goal**: The goal of this project is to deploy a new VM with a default image and then successfully install print services on the virtual machine, using a Custom Script Extension to do so
- **Key commands**:
    - `New-AzureRmResourceGroup`
    - `Get-Credential`
    - `New-AzureRmVm`
    - `Set-AzureRmVmCustomScriptExtension`
    - `Remove-AzureRmResourceGroup`
- **General steps**:
    1. Create a resource group
    2. Deploy a VM with the default image
    3. Install the print server role via Custom Script Extension
    4. Delete the resource group and everything in it after validation
- **Validation**: To confirm that you've completed this project successfully, log in to the virtual machine that you deployed and confirm that the print server is listed as **Installed** in the **Roles** and **Features** wizard
- **Reference information**: The *Custom Script Extensions* section

Resetting an admin password

Microsoft Azure's **infrastructure as a service** (**IaaS**) offering allows the management of virtual machines through a so-called cloud layer. As such, accessing a virtual machine through the OS itself is not necessary when resetting an admin password.

Virtual machines in Azure normally have a small piece of software, called a VM agent, installed on them. The VM agent is installed at the OS level (usually automatically) and communicates with Azure. This allows out-of-band user control over the operating system without needing to touch the OS itself.

Once the VM Agent is installed on a virtual machine, you can manage the local admin password without needing to interact directly with the OS. This can be accomplished via PowerShell, using the `Set-AzureRmVMAccessExtension` command.

By using the `Set-AzureRmVMAccessExtension` command, you can reset the password and reboot the virtual machine so that the change takes effect.

Resetting the password

To reset a local admin password, you need first to define the virtual machine that you need to work with. To do this, you can use the `Get-AzureRmVm` command, coupled with `Set-AzureRmVMAccessExtension`. Run the following four commands to set up the variables needed to reset the admin password on `myVM1`:

```
$resourceGroupName = "VMLab"

$vmName = "myVM1"

$name = "ResetPassword"

$location = "EastUS"
```

Once you've set up the variables using the preceding commands, update the local admin credentials for the virtual machine by running the following command:

```
$creds = Get-Credential
```

When prompted for credentials, supply the existing local admin username but give it a new password.

After supplying the new local admin credentials, run the `Set-AzureRmVMAccessExtension` command to actually set the new credentials on the virtual machine:

```
Set-AzureRmVMAccessExtension `
 -ResourceGroupName $resourceGroupName `
 -VMName $vmName `
 -Name $name `
 -Location $location `
 -Credential $creds `
 -TypeHandlerVersion "2.0"
```

Once this is complete, the username will have a new password! This technique is useful if you're able to authenticate to your Azure subscription but have forgotten the local password on a virtual machine.

Now it's your turn!

- **Project**: Resetting passwords
- **Project goal**: The goal of this project is to successfully reset the password for a local admin account of a virtual machine
- **Key commands**:
    - `New-AzureRmResourceGroup`
    - `Get-Credential`
    - `New-AzureRmVm`
    - `Set-AzureRmVMAccessExtension`
    - `Restart-AzureRmVM`
    - `Remove-AzureRmResourceGroup`

- **General steps**:
    1. Create a resource group
    2. Deploy a virtual machine with a default configuration
    3. Reset the local admin password for the virtual machine
    4. Delete the resource group and all resources
- **Validation**: After resetting the password, ensure that you can log into the virtual machine with the new password
- **Reference information**: The *Resetting an admin password* section

Wrapping up

Now that you have finished all of the exercises in this book, we urge you to remove the VMLab resource group completely so that there aren't any lingering resources racking up Azure charges without you realizing.

So, to remove the VMLab resource group and everything in it, run the following command:

```
Remove-AzureRmResourceGroup -Name VMLab -force
```

Running this command will ensure that the entire VMLab resource group, along with everything within it, is deleted.

Summary

Thank you for reading our book! We sincerely hope that you have picked up some new knowledge and skills. While this Azure PowerShell book isn't meant to be an all-encompassing technical document, it *is* meant to help you develop skills that many other IT professionals do not possess.

By learning skills that your peers do not possess, you are able to set yourself apart from the pack. As such, you put yourself in a position where you can enjoy higher paying jobs and improved chances for promotions. By following the exercises in this book, you are setting yourself up for success as an IT professional.

Additional learning resources

Hopefully you've found this book useful! In addition to this book, there are other learning resources for you to learn new and exciting skills:

- For video demonstrations of many of the exercises in this book, visit `https://www.udemy.com/creating-and-managing-azure-virtual-machines-with-powershell/?couponCode=AZUREBOOK` to view an online course entitled *Creating and Managing Azure Virtual Machines with PowerShell*.
- Visit `https://www.udemy.com/courses/search/?q=azuresrc=ukwranMID=39197 ranEAID=61XL3LgL0o8ranSiteID=61XL3LgL0o8-kvwKK8BCX3kXAR.cvb1jpgsiteID= 61XL3LgL0o8-kvwKK8BCX3kXAR.cvb1jpgLSNPUBID=61XL3LgL0o8` to see what other third-party Azure courses are available on Udemy. However, if you prefer Pluralsight, check out `https://www.pluralsight.com/search?q=azureclickid= QK0SrmX1iVEOUDmxhGT1AVizUkgRDOTiTQz8VU0irgwc=1mpid=1259524utm_source= impactradiusutm_medium=digital_affiliateutm_campaign=1259524aid= 7010a000001xAKZAA2` for the latest Azure courses on that platform instead.

For lots of free Azure learning materials, you can also visit `www.understandingazure.com`.

Be sure also to connect with me on LinkedIn: `https://www.linkedin.com/in/thomas-j-mitchell/`.

Other Books You May Enjoy

If you enjoyed this book, you may be interested in these other books by Packt:

Implementing Azure Solutions – Second Edition
Florian Klaffenbach et al.

ISBN: 978-1-78934-304-5

- Create and manage a Kubernetes cluster in Azure Kubernetes Service (AKS)
- Implement site-to-site VPN and ExpressRoute connections in your environment
- Explore the best practices in building and deploying app services
- Use Telemetry to monitor your Azure Solutions
- Design an Azure IoT solution and learn how to operate in different scenarios
- Implement a Hybrid Azure Design using Azure Stack

Hands-On Linux Administration on Azure
Frederik Vos

ISBN: 978-1-78913-096-6

- Understand why Azure is the ideal solution for your open source workloads
- Master essential Linux skills and learn to find your way around the Linux environment
- Deploy Linux in an Azure environment
- Use configuration management to manage Linux in Azure
- Manage containers in an Azure environment
- Enhance Linux security and use Azure's identity management systems
- Automate deployment with Azure Resource Manager (ARM) and Powershell
- Employ Ansible to manage Linux instances in an Azure cloud environment

Leave a review - let other readers know what you think

Please share your thoughts on this book with others by leaving a review on the site that you bought it from. If you purchased the book from Amazon, please leave us an honest review on this book's Amazon page. This is vital so that other potential readers can see and use your unbiased opinion to make purchasing decisions, we can understand what our customers think about our products, and our authors can see your feedback on the title that they have worked with Packt to create. It will only take a few minutes of your time, but is valuable to other potential customers, our authors, and Packt. Thank you!

Index